The American 45 and 78 RPM Record Dating Guide, 1940-1959

Discographies
Series Editor: Michael Gray

The American 45 and 78 RPM Record Dating Guide, 1940-1959

Compiled by **WILLIAM R. DANIELS**

Discographies, Number 16

Greenwood Press

Westport, Connecticut • London, England

Library of Congress Cataloging in Publication Data

Daniels, William R.
    The American 45 and 78 rpm record dating guide,
1940-1959.

        (Discographies, ISSN 0192-334X ; no. 16)
        Bibliography: p.
        Includes index.
        1. Sound recordings—Chronology.   I. Title.
II. Title: The American forty-five and seventy-eight
rpm record dating guide, 1940-1959.   III.   Series.
ML156.2.D36 1985   789.9'12'0973   84-22420
ISBN 0-313-24232-1 (lib. bdg.)

Library of Congress Catalog Card Number: 84-22420
ISBN: 0-313-24232-1
ISSN: 0192-334X

First published in 1985

Greenwood Press
A division of Congressional Information Service, Inc.
88 Post Road West, Westport, Connecticut 06881

Printed in the United States of America

10 9 8 7 6 5 4 3 2 1

Contents

Acknowledgments

Compilation of this book was made possible through the help
of many people who freely gave support, information, and
ideas. First and foremost I thank Charleen, my wife, for
her patience and encouragement through all phases of this
work. I also thank the staff of the Boston Public Library
for the endless miles they walked bringing me bound volumes
from the stacks and searching for boxes of microfilm for my
use. Thanks are also due a number of people who have been
involved in this project to various degrees through the past
decade or more. Initial encouragement to do the research
came from Art Turco of Record Exchanger magazine. As the
project expanded, Peter Grendysa and the late Rick Whitesell
convinced me that such research was important and useful.
Also entitled to thanks is Steven C. Barr, whose research in
the field of record dating along with his publication The
(Almost) Complete 78 rpm Record Dating Guide gave me inspi-
ration and ideas for formating my work. George Moonoogian
and Victor Pearlin deserve special thanks for their support
and encouragement through the years. Thanks to Al Pavlow
for sending me information regarding late 1940s labels.
       Two persons who deserve unique acknowledgment are
Fernando Gonzalez, who singlehandedly gave me the incentive
for completing the materials on the fifties, and Doug Seroff,
for constant encouragment through the years.
       To Harold Flakser, Galen Gart, Peter Gibbon, Martin
Hawkins, Cedric Hayes, Bob Laughton, and Bob Porter belong
thanks for their ideas and support. A very special word of
thanks goes to Michel Ruppli who suggested that Greenwood
Press might be interested in my manuscript, and Mary R. Sive
of Greenwood Press for her patience and suggestions over the
last year and a half.

Preface

This work makes available to the public a simple-to-use
dating guide for 45 and 78 rpm records released by all United States companies between the years 1940 and 1959. It en-
ables the reader to date the specific month of record release for single issues of almost 2,500 record companies,
a total of 93,000 individual discs.
        I recognized the need for this work in the late
1960s, at that time little information was available regarding the vast number of records issued during the preceding
decades. Initial research for records released in 1956 began in the fall of 1969. The periodical <u>Variety</u> served as
the original source, but I shortly discovered that <u>Billboard</u>,
<u>The Cash Box</u>, and <u>One-Stop</u> magazines listed even more infor-
mation. Dating regarding the Coleman label came from the
<u>Chicago Defender</u>, and one Gotham Record Company catalog was
also consulted. In 1971 I began systematically collecting
information regarding recordings issued during the decade of
the 1950s, and by the mid-1970s I had amassed a considerable
inventory of data. A vacation week in 1980 provided the op-
portunity to begin research on 1940s releases and to consid-
er various methods of presentation. This book is the result
of over fifteen years of effort. The format is based upon
the work of Steven C. Barr <u>The (Almost) Complete 78 rpm Rec-</u>
<u>ord Dating Guide</u> which focuses upon the period 1900 to 1942
and includes information and diagrams regarding the label
styles.
        The following pages list record companies in alpha-
betical order. Subsidiary and related companies are also
listed independentely with cross-references to the name of
the parent company. Thus, under Decca the reader will find
the subsidiaries Coral and Brunswick, and under those names
will be found references to Decca. Punctuation marks are
omitted, and symbols and numbers are alphabetized as though
spelled out. Each company is followed by its release series,
from the lowest to the highest. Errors in the original
sources have been corrected when more reliable information
could be obtained. Variant spellings and title changes are
noted. Companies using the same name are seperated (for ex-
ample: Kangaroo, Spotlight). An Addendum includes last

minute information received too late to incorporate in the
main listing.

The most significant aspect of the <u>Guide</u> is that it
presents information about numerous companies for which no
listings previously existed. It is based upon the assump-
tion that record companies were faithful and prompt in sending out copies of their releases to magazines for listing,
advertising, and review. Since many companies are no longer
in existence and the whereabouts of their files unknown,
listings in periodicals are the only source for the research-
er.

Besides its being an aid to dating records, the
<u>Guide</u> sheds light on the history of specific recording com-
panies and of the history of the recording industry as a
whole. I hope that it will provide the reader with as much
delight as gathering the data gave me. It is also my hope
that the <u>Guide</u> will enhance the interest and enjoyment of
all who collect recordings, research articles, or simply
listen to the recordings of the 1940s and 1950s. Comments
will be welcomed.

Introduction

In 1877 Thomas Edison made the first sound recording by projecting sound onto a tinfoil cylinder. Commercial use of sound recordings began in 1890, and by 1894 the initial flat records resembling those we use today were on the market. Sales of both cylinder and and flat records totaled 25 million by 1914. With the conclusion of World War I, the record industry expanded to 100 million records sold annually. All recordings up to this time were made by the sheer force of a human voice or musical instrument being projected onto the recording medium. By 1927 the process was vastly improved by the use of electronic microphones and amplification.

The recording industry declined sharply during the Depression; small companies faltered, and the majors cut back production drastically. In the late 1930s the industry began to revive, but not until 1941 did total record sales equal previous highs.

In 1940 the recording industry was dominated by Columbia, Decca, and Victor (RCA Victor). A few independents such as Commodore, Blue Note, and Varsity also survived. At that time a number of forces began to effect deep changes in the recording industry. Broadcast Music Incorporated (BMI) was organized in 1940 for the purpose of music being licensing music for public broadcast. This resulted in a much wider selection of music being licensed for public broadcast.

At the same time a number of factors held back the growth of the recording industry. First, a shellac shortage beginning in 1941 hampered production for the next three years. Second, World War II brought with it the drafting of many members of recording groups into the armed forces. Third, and most important, the American Federation of Musicians called a recording strike beginning on July 31, 1942. The union wanted a portion of the price of each record to go into a fund for retired musicians. The strike paralyzed the recording industry. Capitol and Decca conceded in the Autumn of 1943, but Victor and Columbia held out until November, 1944. With the end of the strike came a flood of independent recordings. Record sales doubled from $109 million

in 1945 to $218 million in 1946. The industry received yet
another setback when the second recording strike of the decade began on December 31, 1947,--the industry declined until
the strike ended on December 14, 1948. After rapidly ex-
panding, the industry leveled off and entered a stagnant pe-
riod which lasted until the sales boom of 1956. Three
events of the late 1940s paved the way for that boom: the
availability of magnetic recording tape in August, 1947; the
birth of the microgroove record by Columbia, which made pos-
ible the introduction of long-playing albums in June, 1948;
and the birth of RCA Victor's 45 rpm seven-inch record in
the spring of 1949.

The 1950s saw a battle over the size and speed of
single-issue recordings. The decade began with only a hand-
ful of seven-inch 45 rpm recordings being pressed and ended
with the almost extinction of the ten-inch 78 rpm record.
The discovery of the teenaged consumer created the most
notable change in the sale of records, and in a few short
years the content of popular music changed dramatically to
take advantage of the new market. Between 1954 and 1959
the total income of the recording industry almost tripled.
Additional changes that occured during the decade included
the introduction of the 45 rpm extended-play album in 1953
by RCA; the introduction of long-playing stereo albums in
November, 1957; and the availability of stereo singles of
large-selling recordings by 1959.

From the introduction of the first recordings in
1877 to the end of 1959, the single-issue record dominated
the recording industry. Beginning in the 1960s the dominant form of recording would be the twelve-inch album.

The American
45 and 78 RPM
Record Dating Guide,
1940-1959

The American 45 and 78 RPM Record Dating Guide, 1940-1959

AA

104	2/55
108	5/55
Name Change	

(DOUBLE AA)

114	7/55
116	10/55
117	1/56

AARDELL

1	5/55
2	7/55
4	9/55
5	11/55
6	1/56
8	2/56

ABBEY

A-50	12/48
53	3/49
62	5/49
66	7/49
69	8/49

1246	5/50

3001	9/49
3002	10/49
3008	12/49
3014	4/50
3015	8/50
3021	1/51
3022	3/51
3030	11/51
3031	2/52

5001	11/49

7004	12/49
7006	5/50

9001	10/49

15001	1/50
15003	3/50
15004	4/50
15009	6/50
15011	8/50
15027	11/50
15034	1/51
15039	3/51
15042	4/51
15053	8/51
15062	2/52
15064	4/52
15073	8/52
15075	10/52

ABBOTT

100	11/51
106	12/51
108	3/52
112	4/52
113	1/53
125	3/53
136	5/53
139	6/53
140	8/53
145	9/53
146	11/53
150	12/53
152	2/54
156	3/54
161	4/54

162	5/54
165	7/54
170	9/54
171	10/54
172	11/54
174	12/54
176	2/55
177	3/55
179	5/55
180	7/55
183	8/55
185	10/55
186	1/56
187	7/56
188	11/56
189	12/56
190	2/57

1001	7/54
1002	10/54

3001	8/54
3002	1/55
3003	3/55
3009	8/55
3010	9/55
3011	10/55
3014	11/55
3015	1/56
3016	2/56
3018	3/56
3023	5/56
3024	9/56
3025	12/56
3026	2/57

(FABOR)

100	11/53
103	2/54

ABBOTT (FABOR) CON'T	
104	3/54
106	4/54
108	5/54
110	6/54
111	8/54
113	9/54
117	12/54
118	1/55
120	3/55
121	4/55
123	5/55
128	8/55
129	10/55
130	11/55
135	6/56
137	7/56
140	9/56
142	2/57

2001	7/54

4001	12/54
4002	1/55
4003	4/55
4004	5/55
4006	8/55
4007	10/55
4008	1/56
4011	6/56
4013	9/56
4017	12/56

ABC	
100	3/50

207	6/50

549	9/49

ABC EAGLE	
?	7/49
148	9/49

ABCO	
102	4/56
105	6/56
107	7/56

ABC-PARAMOUNT	
9655	11/55
9665	1/56
9672	2/56
9681	3/56
9700	4/56
9705	5/56
9707	6/56
9718	7/56
9731	8/56
9737	9/56
9745	10/56
9770	11/56
9777	12/56
9778	1/57
9786	2/57
9793	3/57
9809	4/57
9815	5/57
9830	6/57
9835	7/57
9850	8/57
9852	9/57
9857	10/57
9870	11/57
9875	12/57
9882	1/58
9891	2/58
9902	3/58
9910	4/58
9926	5/58
9930	6/58
9940	7/58
9947	8/58
9953	9/58
9967	10/58
9974	11/58
9988	12/58
9993	1/59
10009	3/59
10016	4/59
10019	5/59
10025	6/59
10031	7/59
10036	8/59
10045	9/59
10051	10/59
10064	11/59
10068	12/59

(APT)	
25002	6/58
25006	7/58
25008	8/58
25012	9/58
25014	10/58

25021	11/58
25025	12/58
25027	1/59
25030	3/59
25033	4/59
25034	5/59
25036	6/59

(HUNT)	
318	4/58
323	12/58
324	2/59
325	4/59
327	6/59
328	7/59
336	11/59

(SURE)	
1004	5/59

ABEL	
227	12/59

A-BELL	
409	6/58

524	4/55

606	8/58

825	12/52
830	6/53
841	2/54
890	11/54

ABNER	
(SEE VEE JAY)	

ACADEMY	
50	6/54

100	7/50

1019	4/54

1436	2/59

5558	5/55
5851	10/58

54113	1/55

ACAMA
109   5/55
112   11/55
113   1/59

AC'CENT
1008   2/54
1010   5/54
1012   8/54
1022   11/54
1024   5/55
1027   7/55
1029   8/55
1030   11/55
1034   2/56
1041   5/56
1044   10/56
1046   11/56
1047   4/57
1051   9/57
1060   5/58
1062   8/58
1064   9/58

ACCORDIA
1955   10/50

ACE   (NY)
102   10/56
105   12/56
110   8/57
117   10/57
118   2/58
120   7/58
124   11/58
125   12/58
----
151   9/58
191   8/59

ACE   (MISS.)
505   8/55
512   10/55
514   1/56
518   7/56
521   10/56
524   2/57
529   6/57
530   9/57
538   10/57
541   1/58
546   5/58

553   11/58
554   12/58
555   2/59
558   3/59
561   4/59
562   5/59
566   6/59
569   8/59
571   9/59
572   11/59
576   12/59

(ACE)
5000   5/58
5002   4/59
(SEE ALSO
     ATLANTIC)

(VIN)
1000   5/58
1008   12/58
1010   2/59
1011   3/59
1013   4/59
1014   5/59
1015   6/59

ACE OF FLA.

1001   10/57

ACME
0013   11/49
----
104   5/57
106   6/57
----
713   4/57
718   9/57
----
965   7/51
966   8/51

ACORN
(SEE SAVOY)

AD
101   8/58
103   3/59

ADAM

1033   11/50
1037   12/50
1052   5/53

ADAY
311   8/57
360   6/58

ADDISON
1500   6/59
15002   9/59
15003   10/59

ADELPHI
100   3/57

2011   10/53

ADMIRAL
202   2/50
203   4/50

1001   12/49
1002   1/50
1003   3/50
1004   4/50
1013   6/50
1015   9/50

1004   3/57

ADONIS
102   12/59

A-DORA
1002   2/58

ADVANCE
1000   3/47

2073   9/51

3001   7/55
3002   8/55
3004   9/55
3009   11/55
3011   2/56
3012   3/56
3013   12/56

ADVANCE
CON'T

3015	2/57
3017	4/57
3018	6/57

ADVANCED DISC
120   1/50

ADVENTURE
16   3/50

AETNA
100   6/46
----
301   3/47
----
400   8/47
----
500   3/47

AFS
300   10/57
301   12/57

AFTON
616   6/59

AGE
271   9/58

AGGIE
1001

AGENDA
5601   10/56
5605   12/56

A. H. A.
1001   8/57

AHA
101   8/58

AIR
1003   3/59

AIR LOOM
102   2/58

AIRWAY
104   10/58

ALADDIN
(PHILO)

101	6/45
103	8/45
105	10/45
107	12/45
118	4/46

NAME CHANGE!!
ALADDIN

127	5/46
139	6/46
151	7/46
152	9/46
154	10/46
163	2/47
175	5/47
195	9/47
207	2/48
211	5/48

506	6/46
509	8/46
510	9/46
536	6/47

2001	6/46
2003	1/47
2020	5/48
2028	10/49
2029	2/50
2031	9/50
2035	10/50
2036	3/53
2038	4/53
2039	12/53

3001	5/47
3002	6/47
3007	2/48
3011	5/48
3012	11/48
3020	1/49
3021	2/49
3025	3/49

3027	4/49
3030	7/49
3037	10/49
3039	11/49
3040	12/49
3048	2/50
3053	3/50
3054	4/50
3057	5/50
3059	6/50
3060	7/50
3063	8/50
3066	10/50
3073	11/50
3076	1/51
3079	2/51
3080	3/51
3086	4/51
3087	5/51
3096	6/51
3097	7/51
3103	9/51
3104	10/51
3109	12/51
3116	1/52
3124	2/52
3129	4/52
3130	5/52
3133	6/52
3136	7/52
3144	8/52
3147	9/52
3151	10/52
3155	11/52
3163	1/53
3169	2/53
3174	3/53
3178	4/53
3179	5/53
3191	6/53
3196	7/53
3197	8/53
3201	9/53
3205	10/53
3211	11/53
3214	12/53
3220	1/54
3224	3/54
3229	4/53
3236	5/54
3244	6/54
3248	7/54
3250	8/54
3254	9/54
3261	10/54
3265	11/54

ALADDIN
CON'T

3270	12/54
3272	2/55
3279	3/55
3285	4/55
3292	7/55
3293	8/55
3299	10/55
3303	11/55
3312	1/56
3313	2/56
3316	3/56
3318	4/56
3320	5/56
3321	6/56
3329	8/56
3334	9/56
3337	10/56
3340	11/56
3351	12/56
3352	1/57
3357	2/57
3367	3/57
3372	4/57
3374	5/57
3381	6/57
3383	7/57
3390	8/57
3391	9/57
3400	11/57
3401	12/57
3408	1/58
3412	3/58
3416	5/58
3428	6/58
3431	7/58
3442	8/58
3444	12/58
3445	1/59
3449	3/59
3452	4/59
3456	5/59
3458	6/59
3460	9/59
3461	11/59
3463	2/60
3466	8/60
3467	9/60

(SCORE)

4002	6/48
4005	11/48
4008	10/49

5002	5/48
5007	5/49
5009	7/49
5011	11/49
5015	2/50
5020	7/50
5022	8/50
5023	10/50
5025	2/51
5031	8/51
5032	9/51
5035	4/52
5039	4/53
5040	6/53
5055	7/54
5056	3/55

(INTRO)

6001	4/50
6002	7/50
6003	9/50
6005	2/51
6012	3/51
6013	4/51
6016	5/51
6018	6/51
6023	7/51
6024	9/51
6031	11/51
6033	12/51
6037	1/52
6042	2/52
6043	3/52
6050	4/52
6054	5/52
6057	7/52
6058	9/52
6062	11/52
6065	2/53
6068	3/53
6071	4/53
6072	6/53
6076	7/53
6078	8/53
6083	10/53
6086	3/54
6088	4/54
6089	11/55
6091	12/55
6092	7/56
6094	11/56
6097	8/57

7012	8/54

9000	7/58

(LAMP)

2002	3/57
2005	5/57

8001	7/54
8006	11/54

9001	7/54

(ORFEO)

?	11/51
?	10/52

(7-11)

2100	3/53
2103	6/53

(ULTRA)

51	10/54

101	2/56

NAME CHANGE
TO: (DIG)

106	4/56
111	6/56
115	8/56
118	9/56
120	10/56
125	12/56
134	5/57
138	6/57

ALANA
555 11/58

ALBA
416 7/54

ALBEN
501 11/48

2002	3/49

AL-BRITE
1300 12/59

ALDON
100 3/56

ALERT
200   8/46
207   5/48
----
400   5/46
401   8/46
413   5/48

ALEXANDER
A-100   10/49

2370   9/53
2376   7/55

ALGENE
1955   7/48

ALGONQUIN
1001   4/52

ALHUMBRA
370   9/58

ALL
501   12/58
502   5/59

ALLAN
107   2/59
108   5/59
----
903   3/50

ALLEGRO
101   6/48
----
752   11/48

ALLEN
100   7/53
----
227   4/53
230   5/53
232   6/53
233   8/53
239   11/53

1000   6/53

21000   6/49
21001   8/49

ALLIED
5000   4/53
5002   4/53
5003   7/53
5006   8/53
5009   11/53
5019   3/54
5021   4/54
5024   5/54

7778   10/59

10000   4/58
10010   3/59

ALL STAR
7100   11/53
7162   7/57
7167   8/58
7169   9/58
7172   11/58
7174   1/59
7179   3/59
7181   4/59
7185   5/59
7186   6/59
7188   7/59
7189   8/59
7190   9/59
7193   11/59
----
501   3/58

ALMA
51   12/53
----
81   4/54

ALPHA
A-2   10/46

1001   6/46
1002   4/48

2003   11/52

122-6   4/46

ALPINE
SEE COLUMBIA

ALTON
254   9/59
----
600   11/59

ALVA
53   7/54

ALVEN
1650   6/51

ALVINA
688   6/54

AMANDA
1001   12/59

AMBASSADOR
281   6/47
297   8/47

1003   1/52
1005   11/53
1007   3/54

AMERICAN
44   1/50
----
100   3/53
106   4/54
111   4/55

1001   12/45

1030   6/56

1000   9/58
1001   10/58

2001   5/46

5001   11/49
5005   11/52

AMERICAN
BEAUTY
778   10/59

AMERICAN
INTERNATIONAL
532   6/59
543   10/59
545   12/59

AMIJO
929   5/53

AMMOR
100   3/40

AMP
790   1/59

1001   7/55

32001   1/58

AMPS
129   9/57

1004   2/58
1006   8/58

A NATURAL HIT
101   3/47
103   7/49

ANCHOR
A-1   1/52
3   3/52
A-6   8/52
14   11/52
20   8/53
26   5/55
140   11/57
143   1/58

ANDEX
SEE KEENE

ANDIE
SEE LAURIE

ANDOLL
5210   9/54

ANDREA
101   6/56

ANGLE TONE
SEE ATLAS

ANIMAL
174   2/49

ANNA
102   4/59

1104   4/59
1108   12/59

ANTHONY
501   10/55

ANTHRACITE
102   5/54

ANTLER
4000   8/56
4001   11/56
4005   5/57
4007   10/57
4008   11/57
4009   3/58
4010   5/58
----
842   1/59

1101   3/59
1103   4/59
1105   5/59

A-1
813   6/49
847   8/49

1001   7/44

1004   6/45
1005   2/46
1006   6/47

APACHE
1001   10/55
1004   5/57

APEX
SEE GOTHAM

APEX
951   5/59

7750   4/59
7751   6/59
7753   9/59

76185   9/57

APOLLO
104   3/46
106   4/46
107   5/46
108   8/46
109   10/46
112   12/46
116   2/47
124   3/47
141   4/47
143   5/47
147   6/47
150   7/47
155   9/47
163   10/47
164   12/47
176   1/48
182   4/48
187   7/48
192   10/48
193   11/48
196   1/49
201   3/49
204   4/49
209   6/49
211   7/49
212   8/49
214   11/49
218   12/49
222   4/50
224   5/50
235   11/50

245	9/51	396	2/48	521	2/58
253	1/52	398	4/48	524	3/58
258	4/52	400	9/48	525	5/58
262	6/52	401	11/48	527	11/58
265	9/52	402	1/49	530	1/59
266	10/52	405	3/49	532	2/59
267	12/52	406	5/49	533	3/59
269	2/53	409	8/49	534	4/59
272	3/53	413	10/49	538	10/59
273	7/53	414	11/49	540	11/59
275	9/53	416	12/49	---------	
278	11/53	417	2/50	751	4/44
279	12/53	418	4/50	753	5/44
281	3/54	421	5/50	754	5/45
282	4/54	423	1/51	755	10/45
283	5/54	427	6/51	756	1/46
284	6/54	429	8/51	759	6/46
287	8/54	430	9/51	761	8/46
289	9/54	432	11/51	762	11/46
291	1/55	435	1/52	764	12/46
293	4/55	436	3/52	766	3/47
295	5/55	439	6/52	771	6/47
296	6/55	440	7/52	773	10/47
297	7/55	441	9/52	774	12/47
298	8/55	443	12/52	777	1/48
299	9/55	446	4/53	780	4/48
300	10/55	447	6/53	781	9/48
303	2/56	448	8/53	783	12/48
304	6/56	449	10/53	791	5/49
305	10/56	451	1/54	793	6/49
306	11/56	453	2/54	795	7/49
308	3/57	454	4/54	796	11/49
309	4/57	456	7/54	799	2/50
312	4/58	461	9/54	800	3/50
---------		463	11/54	802	4/50
348	11/44	465	12/54	803	5/50
359	3/45	467	2/55	804	7/50
362	10/45	470	3/55	805	11/50
364	11/45	471	4/55	806	1/51
365	12/45	474	6/55	807	2/51
368	3/46	479	9/55	808	5/51
370	4/46	481	11/55	809	6/51
371	5/46	483	12/55	810	1/52
372	6/46	484	2/56	812	5/52
374	8/46	489	3/56	813	7/52
375	11/46	490	4/56	814	12/52
377	12/46	494	5/56	815	4/53
379	1/47	496	6/56	816	8/53
380	2/47	497	9/56	817	12/53
384	4/47	504	11/56	818	3/54
385	5/47	505	12/56	819	4/54
389	7/47	506	2/57	820	5/54
391	10/47	511	4/57	822	7/54
392	11/47	513	7/57	823	8/54
393	1/48	516	10/57	824	10/55
		520	12/57	825	7/56

APOLLO CON'T
761   7/62

1001   5/46
1007   6/46
1018   8/46
1019   10/46
1022   11/46
1025   1/47
1030   2/47
1041   3/47
1046   4/47
1061   5/47
1069   7/47
1074   8/47
1079   9/47
1080   10/47
1084   11/47
1089   1/48
1094   2/48
1112   3/48
1120   4/48
1122   6/48
1126   8/48
1131   9/48
1140   11/48
1143   4/49
1146   5/49
1148   6/49
1149   7/49
1150   8/49
1156   3/50
1159   5/50
1163   6/50
1166   7/50
1168   10/50
1170   11/50
1175   12/50
1178   1/51
1180   4/51
1184   5/51
1190   3/52
1191   5/52
1194   7/52

(DOE)
101   2/58
107   6/59

(HILL &
   COUNTRY)
104   1/50
105   4/50
111   6/50

(LLOYDS)
101   6/53
102   8/53
104   9/53
105   12/53
109   4/54
110   6/54
113   9/54
114   10/54

(TIMELY)
101   10/53
105   7/54

1003   10/53
1005   4/54
1007   7/54
1008   8/54
1009   11/54
1010   12/54

APON
2142   6/59

APT
SEE ABC-P.

A. P. V.
201   12/57

ARA
118   3/45
120   6/45
134   3/46
137   4/46
161   8/46

3001   3/45

4001   3/45
4003   9/45
4004   10/45

ARC
3000   7/56

4444   6/58
4446   2/59
4447   3/59
4450   6/59

4782   7/56

8001   7/56
8004   12/56

A. R. C.
596   3/59
597   6/59

ARCADE
101   2/52
102   4/52
103   7/52
106   10/52
108   11/52
111   4/53
112   5/53
114   6/53
115   9/53
122   12/53
123   3/54
124   4/54
125   6/54
132   10/54
134   3/55
141   7/56
142   12/56
143   2/57
144   6/57
146   6/58
149   9/58
152   11/58
153   5/59

ARCADIA
110   11/56
111   3/57
114   3/58
116   4/59

1001   9/51

1947   11/47
1948   12/47
1949   8/48
1950   10/48
1951   10/49

2032   1/48

2150   8/48

2545   2/53

ARCH		1001	12/47	5261	12/56
1606	11/58	--------		5262	2/57
1608	1/59	1101	12/47	5266	3/57
1610	3/59	1103	6/48	5268	5/57
		1104	10/48	5272	7/57
		1105	2/49	5278	9/57
ARCO		1106	7/49	5279	10/57
SEE REGIS		1107	11/49	5283	11/57
		--------		5286	1/58
		1202	12/47	5290	2/58
ARCO		--------		5294	4/58
4623	5/58	1301	5/48	5297	5/58
		1305	6/48	5301	6/58
		1307	2/49	5304	7/58
ARGO		1310	7/49	5309	8/58
SEE		1311	11/49	5311	9/58
ARISTOCRAT		--------		5317	10/58
		1401	5/48	5318	11/58
		--------		5320	1/59
ARIES		1701	3/48	5327	2/59
1014	7/56	--------		5329	3/59
		1801	4/48	5331	4/59
		1803	9/48	5335	5/59
ARISTA		--------		5338	6/59
5021	10/46	1901	3/49	5341	8/59
--------		--------		5346	10/59
6001	1/47	2001	4/48	5353	11/59
		2002	10/48	5354	12/59
		2003	2/49	--------	
ARISTOCRAT		--------		(CHECKER)	
101	5/47	2301	11/49	750	4/52
104	7/47	--------		758	8/52
--------		3001	4/49	762	9/52
202	6/47	3002	9/49	764	11/52
--------		--------		765	12/52
401	9/47	3101	1/49	768	1/53
402	11/47	--------		770	4/53
404	1/50	7001	5/49	773	5/53
409	2/50	--------		778	7/53
--------		7113	5/49	781	8/53
501	11/47	--------		782	10/53
505	1/48	8001	6/49	786	12/53
508	2/48	--------		790	1/54
509	4/48	10001	5/49	791	3/54
510	11/48	--------		794	5/54
--------		11001	7/49	796	6/54
603	5/48	--------		799	8/54
604	8/48	(MARTERRY)		801	10/54
605	10/48	5249	2/56	804	11/54
606	11/48	NAME CHANGE:		808	12/54
--------		(ARGO)		810	2/55
801	11/47	5252	4/56	812	3/55
803	8/48	5255	7/56	814	4/55
811	8/49	5257	9/56	817	5/55
--------		5258	10/56	818	6/55
902	7/48			820	7/55

ARISTOCRAT
(CHECKER)
CON'T

823	9/55
826	11/55
829	12/55
830	1/56
832	2/56
833	3/56
834	4/56
835	5/56
840	6/56
845	9/56
846	10/56
849	12/56
854	1/57
856	2/57
859	3/57
860	4/57
863	5/57
864	6/57
865	7/57
872	8/57
873	9/57
875	10/57
880	11/57
885	1/58
886	3/58
892	4/58
894	5/58
895	6/58
900	7/58
902	9/58
904	10/58
910	12/58
912	1/59
914	2/59
919	3/59
921	4/59
923	5/59
925	6/59
929	7/59
931	8/59
934	9/59
935	10/59
936	11/59
939	12/59

(CHESS)

1425	6/50
1458	4/51
1464	6/51
1471	7/51
1475	8/51
1479	9/51
1481	10/51

1488	11/51
1490	12/51
1496	2/52
1500	3/52
1512	5/52
1513	6/52
1525	8/52
1526	11/52
1535	2/53
1539	4/53
1541	5/53
1542	6/53
1543	7/53
1546	8/53
1550	10/53
1552	11/53
1554	12/53
1558	1/54
1560	2/54
1562	3/54
1564	4/54
1566	5/54
1573	6/54
1575	7/54
1576	9/54
1577	10/54
1580	11/54
1582	12/54
1583	1/55
1587	2/55
1588	3/55
1593	4/55
1597	5/55
1598	6/55
1599	7/55
1605	9/55
1607	10/55
1611	12/55
1615	1/56
1618	2/56
1619	3/56
1620	4/56
1626	5/56
1629	6/56
1630	7/56
1632	9/56
1641	11/56
1644	12/56
1647	1/57
1648	2/57
1651	3/57
1658	5/57
1659	6/57
1664	7/57
1670	9/57
1671	10/57

1672	11/57
1678	12/57
1681	2/58
1685	3/58
1689	4/58
1692	5/58
1693	6/58
1699	8/59
1705	9/58
1707	11/58
1713	12/58
1716	1/59
1718	2/59
1720	3/59
1724	4/59
1728	5/59
1729	6/59
1731	7/59
1736	8/59
1738	10/59
1743	11/59
1745	12/59

4858	6/54
4859	9/54
4860	10/54
4863	4/55

ARKAY
1001	10/47

ARLAN
502	1/59

ARLINGTON
201	3/49

301	3/49

ARMAND
1001	4/57

ARNETT
701	6/55
702	3/56

ARNO
3539	7/58

ARROW
712   12/56
714   5/57
715   6/57
718   10/57
720   11/57
724   2/58
732   5/58
737   10/58

1003   3/57
1006   10/57
1008   11/57

(BOW)
300   5/58
308   10/58

ARS
1001   2/56

ART
150   4/55
160   3/56
161   5/56
170   7/58
----
200   8/52

ART-DISC
250   3/53
252   5/53

ARTIC
102   5/59

ARTIST
1001   5/51

1247   6/51
1259   8/51
1421   8/54
1430   9/54
1450   9/56
1459   5/57

ARTISTIC
1500   8/58
1503   3/59
1504   4/59

ARVEE
548   5/59
562   7/59
573   9/59
585   12/59

ARVID
7050   10/46

ARVIS
101   12/59

ARWIN
107   3/58
109   5/58
110   6/58
111   7/58
112   8/58
113   9/58
114   10/58
115   11/58
118   1/59
119   3/59

1001   5/59
1002   6/59
1003   7/59
1004   9/59
1005   12/59

ASA
1003   9/50
1010   12/50

ASH
100   5/44
----
161   10/44
----
344   8/44
347   1/45
352   2/45
357   4/45
359   9/45
361   11/45
----
450   7/44
457   7/45
----
500   5/44
----

551   12/44
560   11/45
----
606   1/46

60061 1/46

(STINSON)
345   10/47
----
367   5/46
----
453   10/47
----
606   6/47
----
701   6/47
703   1/48

(DISC)
501   3/46
----
565   12/47
----
607   1/48
----
879   7/48

2001   3/46
2005   8/46

2500   1/48

3001   2/46

4001   2/46

5086   1/48

6064   3/47
6080   1/48
(FOLKWAYS)
201   5/59
202   10/59

ASR
502   1/50

ATHENIAN
001   12/50
002   3/51

ATHENS
700	8/57
703	12/57
704	2/58

ATKAN
001	8/51

ATLANTIC
662	9/49
664	11/49
665	12/49
666	1/50
670	6/50
671	7/50
674	2/51
675	3/51
677	7/52

721	10/49
722	12/49
723	3/50
724	5/50
725	7/50
726	9/50

852	1/48
854	2/48
855	4/48
861	6/48
862	10/48
867	12/48
868	1/49
869	2/49
871	3/49
874	4/49
876	5/49
877	7/49
880	8/49
881	9/49
882	10/49
889	11/49
891	1/50
895	2/50
900	3/50
905	4/50
907	5/50
910	6/50
917	8/50
922	11/50
926	1/51
928	2/51
932	3/51
937	5/51

941	6/51
943	8/51
948	11/51
954	1/52
960	3/52
964	5/52
967	6/52
971	8/52
976	9/52
980	12/52
984	1/53
989	2/53
990	4/53
994	5/53
997	6/53
1001	8/53
1005	9/53
1008	10/53
1011	11/53
1015	12/53
1018	1/54
1020	2/54
1023	4/54
1029	5/54
1033	6/54
1034	7/54
1039	9/54
1043	11/54
1045	12/54
1049	1/55
1052	2/55
1057	4/55
1063	6/55
1068	7/55
1072	8/55
1074	10/55
1079	12/55
1082	2/56
1088	3/56
1092	4/56
1094	5/56
1099	7/56
1102	8/56
1105	9/56
1111	10/56
1114	11/56
1119	12/56
1123	1/57
1127	3/57
1133	4/57
1138	5/57
1144	6/57
1148	7/57
1152	9/57
1160	10/57
1165	12/57

1170	1/58
1174	2/58
1177	3/58
1181	4/58
1186	5/58
1188	6/58
1193	7/58
1194	8/58
1199	9/58
2003	10/58
2004	11/58
2009	12/58
2011	1/59
2013	2/59
2018	3/59
2023	4/59
2025	5/59
2031	6/59
2033	7/59
2034	8/59
2037	9/59
2041	10/59
2044	11/59
2045	12/59

3001	5/52
3003	10/52
3005	2/54
3009	12/55

15001	8/53
15002	2/54

(ATCO)
6050	9/55
6055	10/55
6060	1/56
6063	2/56
6066	3/56
6069	6/56
6073	7/56
6074	8/56
6076	9/56
6081	12/56
6085	1/57
6086	2/57
6087	3/57
6090	5/57
6092	6/57
6093	7/57
6095	8/57
6099	9/57
6103	7/57
6103	10/57
6106	11/57
6108	1/58

ATLANTIC
(ATCO)
CON'T

6109	2/58
6110	3/58
6115	5/58
6118	6/58
6122	8/58
6123	9/58
6130	11/58
6131	12/58
6132	1/59
6134	2/59
6137	3/59
6140	4/59
6142	6/59
6144	7/59
6146	8/59
6148	9/59
6150	10/59
6152	11/59
6154	12/59

(CAT)

101	4/54
105	7/54
106	8/54
109	9/54
110	12/54
113	4/55
117	10/55

(EAST-WEST)

100	10/57
105	1/58
106	2/58
109	3/58
112	5/58
115	7/58
118	8/58
121	12/58
123	2/59

(KRC)

?	2/57
301	7/57
302	10/57
304	3/58
SEE ACE	

(SPARK)

101	4/54
103	6/54
105	8/54
107	10/54
108	12/54

113	4/55
114	5/55
117	6/55
119	8/55
120	9/55

(TREY)

101	11/59

3000	11/59

(PLAZA)

5502	10/49

ATLAS

1	12/50

100	10/44
104	6/45
107	7/45
113	8/45
119	4/46
122	9/46
127	11/46
142	6/47
147	10/47
153	12/47
155	7/48
158	11/48

1001	1/52
1004	3/52
1007	7/52
1023	8/52
1026	2/53
1028	5/53
1031	8/53
1033	10/53
1038	12/54
1039	6/55
1050	9/55
1051	1/56
1052	3/56
1068	5/56
1069	10/56
1071	2/57
1072	4/57
1075	5/57
1086	9/57
1090	5/58
1092	8/58
1103	1/59

2700	6/57

(ANGLE TONE)

502	4/55
507	12/55
520	11/57
525	5/58
530	11/58
538	10/58

ATOMIC

101	3/57

201	1/46
220	2/46
230	3/46
236	4/46
240	5/46
250	8/46
260	2/47

1002	7/49
1003	1/50
1005	3/50
1010	5/52

2003	2/50

A. T. V.

8152	3/53

AUDICON

102	8/59
104	10/59

AUDITION

1501	9/57

AUDIOVOX

101	5/53
103	8/53
105	12/53
106	1/54
107	3/54
108	7/54
111	11/54
114	1/55
115	4/55
116	7/55

AUR

6661	9/58

AURORA
1954   9/59

AUTHENTIC
403   9/56
410   1/57
- - - - - - - - -
701   6/56
703   7/56

AUTOGRAPH
811   10/49
817   6/50
- - - - - - - - -
2001   7/47

A-V
5401   7/58

AVALANCHE
1001   8/58
1002   1/59

AVALON
7211   4/53
- - - - - - - - -
63707   7/54
63712   12/55

AVANT
065   8/59
074   9/59

AVENUE
6372   11/57

AVIS
111   11/53
114   12/53

AVON
701   6/47

AWARD
129   7/59
- - - - - - - - -

151   8/59
- - - - - - - - -
1023   11/58

AWARE
122   12/58
126   3/59

AZELEA
002   12/54
016   7/55
- - - - - - - - -
106   1/56
107   3/56
109   9/56
111   8/58
116   2/59
121   9/59

AZURE
4301   6/57

BACCHANAL
2001   5/50

BACK BAY
110   5/50

BACK BEAT
SEE PEACOCK

BAKERSFIELD
104   8/56
109   2/57
119   5/57
121   6/57
129   7/57
130   12/57
131   2/58
133   12/58
- - - - - - - - -
502   8/56

BALBOA
0001   3/56
0002   8/56
0003   10/56
0004   2/57

0006   7/57
0008   8/59
0009   12/59

BALD EAGLE
5   4/59
- - - - - - - - -
1002   12/56
- - - - - - - - -
3001   2/58

BALE
101   12/58

BALLAD
1000   9/53
1008   7/55
1013   11/55

BALLY
1000   2/56
1002   3/56
1003   4/56
1006   5/56
1013   7/56
1016   9/56
1018   10/56
1020   11/56
1022   12/56
1026   2/57
1029   3/57
1031   4/57
1034   5/57
1036   6/57
1038   7/57
1043   8/57
1055   9/57

BALOR
2001   9/58

BAMA
100   2/50
103   3/50
105   4/50
- - - - - - - - -
201   7/50
202   3/51
- - - - - - - - -
300   6/50

BAMA CON'T

301	2/51

2101	6/51
2103	7/51

2200	6/51

BANA
523	10/57

BANANA
502	11/57
509	1/58

BANDERA
1301	8/58
1302	12/58
1303	1/59
1304	8/59

2503	4/59
2505	5/59

B&F
SEE UNITED

BANDLAND
10003	2/52

BANDWAGON
401	5/48

505	6/48

BANNER
382	9/50

501	2/47
511	9/47
518	2/48
523	3/48
559	4/48
564	9/48
568	11/48
580	2/50
583	10/50

2001	1/47
2007	5/58

2101	9/50

BARB
100	4/58
101	12/58

BARBOUR
451	8/53
452	11/53

BARCLAY
1303	7/55
1304	10/55
1305	11/55
1306	2/56
1308	5/56
1309	6/56
1314	8/56

BARNABY COAST
1001	8/58

BARRY
712	11/52

812	3/53

BART
21	7/57

BARTHEL
210	2/50

BATON
200	3/54
201	5/54
203	10/54
207	12/54
208	2/55
209	3/55
210	6/55
213	8/55
215	11/55
218	12/55
219	2/56

222	3/56
225	5/56
227	6/56
228	9/56
230	10/56
235	3/57
238	5/57
242	6/57
245	7/57
246	8/57
248	10/57
249	11/57
251	2/58
252	3/58
253	4/58
255	6/58
258	8/58
261	9/58
262	10/58
264	12/58
266	1/59
269	5/59
(SIR)	
270	7/59
271	8/59
272	10/59
274	11/59
(BATON)	
302	5/54

5308	10/54

BAYOU
SEE IMPERIAL

BAYOU
703	9/59

BAY-TONE
101	11/58

BBS
101	5/52
106	10/52
109	2/53
116	6/53
119	8/53
121	9/53
126	5/54
136	7/54

5000	6/53

BBS CON'T
5002	7/53

(BURGUNDY)
1	8/54

106	12/54

BEA & BABY
101	9/59

BEACON
102	8/42
104	9/42
107	12/42
109	1/43
110	2/43
111	4/43
112	5/43
117	11/43

104	12/54

463	1/59

5001	5/43
5002	6/43
5003	12/43
5021	10/47

7001	8/43
7004	9/43
7013	12/43
7120	1/44
7121	2/44

7210	10/47

9131	3/51
9133	5/51
9139	10/51
9143	3/52
9146	5/52

(CELEBRITY)
2003	2/48
2006	3/48
2011	4/48

4000	2/48

7120	6/50

(DAVIS)
442	10/55
443	12/55
444	2/56
446	4/56
447	6/56
452	9/56
454	10/56

2101	3/46
2105	4/46
2107	5/46
2110	11/46

5108	5/46

7017	4/46

7103	3/46

9000	11/46

(JAY DEE)
666	5/54

777	7/53
780	9/53
781	10/53
785	1/54
790	3/54
792	6/54
793	8/54
794	10/54
797	1/55
800	4/55
803	5/55
804	6/55
810	2/56

889	5/54
890	10/54

1100	6/54

(JOE DAVIS)
3520	6/45

3601	9/45
3606	12/45

3901	5/45

4500	6/45

5006	3/45
5008	8/45

5016	9/45
5021	11/45

5102	4/45
5103	8/45
5107	11/45

6666	11/45

7000	4/45
7013	6/45

7126	3/45
7133	5/45
7136	9/45

7153	6/45
7155	11/45

7175	2/45

7192	3/45

7200	8/45
7205	9/45
7207	11/45

7220	2/45

7620	1/45

7777	6/45

8002	8/45
8003	11/45

8129	8/45
8131	9/45

8191	8/45

8250	6/45
8251	8/45

8888	6/45

8900	6/45

BEAM
707	7/57

BEAT
582	5/58

B. E. A. T.
1001   3/59

BEE
1102   2/58
1106   3/58
1109   6/58
1113   3/59

BEECH
711   8/56
713   9/56

BEE HIVE
1314   12/58

BEL-AIR
6082   8/59

BEL CANTO
03   9/58
----
722   8/58
726   11/58
727   2/59

BELDA
106   12/50

BEL-KAY
600   4/58

BELL
108   10/53
----
432   10/43
507   2/48

1002   3/47
1004   10/53
1012   11/53
1022   12/53
1027   2/54
1029   3/54
1034   5/54
1043   6/54
1053   10/54
1074   12/54

1087   4/55
1093   5/55
1096   6/55
1101   11/55
1109   12/55
1113   1/56

5065   8/54
5286   12/56

8912   1/55

BELLA
15   5/59
16   8/59
17   9/59
----
56   4/57

2206   1/59
2210   4/59
2212   6/59

BELLE
565   10/48
----
711   1/56

1001   2/53

2051   10/53

2275   10/53

3456   1/54

4443   4/55

5551   4/55

7777   5/55

BELMONT
16   8/53
----
101   4/50

BEL-TONE
255   8/45
257   9/45
259   11/45
268   2/46

751   3/46
762   6/46

7001   2/46
7012   9/46

BELVEDERE
205   12/50

3001   2/51

4002   3/51
4003   6/51

BENAL
1   4/54

BENIDA
2011   3/54
2087   7/54

5004   11/53
5008   3/54
5016   7/54
5018   9/54
5020   11/54
5025   12/54
5029   4/55
5031   5/55
5032   6/55
5034   7/55

BENNETT
401   8/49

BERGEN
100   12/56

(WANGER)
186   8/58

BERNICE
202   12/58

BERNLO
1001   4/57

BERWICK
2756   10/56

BEST
1003   5/59

BETA
1002   2/59
1003   4/59
1007   8/59

BETHLEHEM
52   3/56

1291   3/54
1297   6/54
1298   9/54
1306   7/55

11001   9/58
11003   11/58
11011   12/58
11012   1/59
11015   2/59
11020   4/59
11021   6/59
11052   9/59
11055   11/59

BG
101   2/52

BIBLETONE
301   8/45
----
773   2/51

1010   3/53
1012   6/53
1013   8/53

1510   6/53
1511   8/53
1513   2/54

2005   2/50

2019   10/48

2101   3/50
2111   5/53

2112   6/53
2115   2/54

2201   2/50

2302   7/50

2401   7/50

3003   2/50
3015   4/53
3016   6/53
3017   9/53

3510   6/53
3511   10/53

4010   7/52
4012   10/52
4014   6/53

4510   10/53

5017   6/53
5018   8/53
5022   10/54

5510   9/53

6011   12/50
6029   2/53
6031   5/53
6032   6/53
6033   8/53
6034   10/53

6051   2/52

6510   10/53

7009   2/50
7025   11/50
7032   4/52
7034   5/52
7035   6/52
7037   10/52
7038   1/53
7039   3/53
7040   6/53
7041   8/53
7042   10/53

8003   4/52
8006   5/52
8007   8/52
8008   9/52

8011   3/53
8013   5/53
8014   6/53
8018   12/53
8020   5/54

8852   3/55
8856   10/55

9017   5/52
9023   9/54

9102   9/54

BIBLICAL
200   12/56

BIG
602   5/55
603   8/55
604   12/55
607   5/57
609   8/57
610   10/57
613   11/57
614   3/58
617   4/58
618   5/58

BIG BANG
1012   6/58
1013   7/58
1015   11/58
1017   12/58
1018   3/59

BIG BAND
1001   8/57

BIG BEN
1578   10/58

BIG D
711

BIGELOW
3578   11/54
3579   12/54

BIG HOWDY
777   5/59

7779   12/59

BIG NICKEL
1001   6/50
1002   7/50
1005   9/50
1009   12/50

BIG RED
101   8/58

BIG-TIME
100   10/56

BIG TOP
3001   6/58
3003   7/58
3004   9/58
3007   2/59
3015   6/59
3026   8/59
3029   10/59
3031   11/59

BIG TOWN
SEE FOUR STAR

BIG WHEEL
100   10/52

BLACK AND
            WHITE
7   9/44
9   6/45
14   8/45
----
100   8/45
102   9/45
107   12/45
108   9/46
109   11/46
113   1/47
117   2/47
118   4/47
119   5/47
121   6/47

122   11/47
123   1/48
124   3/48
125   4/48
126   5/48
127   7/48
----
150   12/48
151   3/49
----
200   4/46
202   5/48
----
301   9/46
----
557   3/48
----
750   11/45
760   1/46
769   3/46
778   4/46
780   5/46
783   6/49
785   7/46
788   7/46
792   9/46
796   10/46
819   12/46
825   1/47
827   2/47
834   4/47
835   5/47
849   6/47
850   8/47
854   12/47
855   1/48
857   3/48
859   4/48
862   5/48
871   3/49
872   5/49
873   7/49

1004   3/46
1007   7/46

1204   1/45

2005   7/46
2008   8/46
2009   10/46

3001   7/46
3004   8/46
3007   11/46

3501   6/45
3506   2/47

3814   5/48

4000   10/46
4007   3/48
4008   7/48

7509   6/46
7510   7/46

10000   11/45
10010   11/46
10017   2/47
10019   6/47
10021   8/47
10023   1/48
10025   4/48

(COMET)
1-A   6/44

C-1   10/44

T-4   7/45

T-50   9/48
T-52   2/49
T-53   3/49

T-100   12/48
----
400   5/44

BLACK DOG
4610   5/55
4613   10/55

BLACK GOLD
100   3/57
103   3/59
105   4/59
106   5/59

BLACK STONE
541   4/54

BLAZE
101   5/59
----
349   9/49

BLUE
101   6/49
106   7/49
113   2/51
119   3/51
127   9/51
129   11/51
130   3/52
134   8/52

(DOOTONE)
301   12/51
304   1/52
305   2/52
310   7/52
315   11/52
335   4/54
338   5/54
342   7/54
345   8/54
347   9/54
357   1/55
358   2/55
36   4/55
364   6/55
367   7/55
370   9/55
372   10/55
377   11/55
380   12/55
381   1/56
384   2/56
393   4/56
395   5/56
396   6/56
400   8/56
404   10/56
407   11/56
409   12/56
410   1/57

(DOOTO)
412   3/57
414   5/57
417   6/57
422   8/57
428   10/57
429   12/57
432   1/58
433   2/58
434   3/58
437   5/58
438   6/58
441   9/58
446   3/59
451   8/59

1201   12/53

BLUE BELL
1041   11/58

BLUEBIRD
SEE RCA
        VICTOR

BLUE BONNET
101   2/59
107   5/59
----
201   4/59
----
701   5/59
710   11/59

1501   5/59

2001   5/59
2002   8/59

4051   5/59

BLUE BONNET
132   2/48
136   5/48
141   7/48

BLUE CHIP
102   3/49

BLUE CHIP
0001   3/57
0013   5/57

BLUE CIRCLE
501   10/53

BLUE FEATHER
294   6/59

BLUE HEN
117   5/57
118   3/59
----

200   3/55
206   5/55
207   6/55
208   8/55
209   9/55
211   12/55
218   5/56
222   6/56
224   11/56
226   4/57
227   7/57
230   7/58
231   12/58
232   3/59
234   6/59

3001   10/52

BLUE JAY
2001   11/54

BLUE LAKE
108   1/55
113   7/55

BLUE MILL
110   3/48
----
201   3/48

BLUE MILL
102   12/52
104   8/53
105   11/53
109   5/54
120   3/56
122   4/57

BLUE MOON
58   12/58
----
411   2/59
412   4/59
414   7/59

5887   9/56

BLUE MOUNTAIN
295   1/50

BLUE NOTE
31   5/44
34   9/44
36   12/44
40   5/45
48   12/45
49   1/48
54   2/49
----
510   11/45
517   8/46
522   1/47
534   4/47
536   7/47
537   10/47
539   11/47
542   1/48
547   6/48
553   12/48
554   2/49
560   6/49
566   10/49
567   1/50

1267   11/49

1568   1/50
1577   7/51
1580   10/51
1589   4/52
1590   5/52
1593   6/52
1594   8/52
1598   11/52
1605   4/53
1621   5/54
1627   6/54
1638   5/56
1668   8/57
1677   1/58
1693   5/58
1708   10/58
1722   11/58
1728   12/58
1736   4/59
1740   5/59
1748   8/59

BLUE RIBBON
7   6/50

1925   1/55

BLUE STAR
1000   7/45

25-25   2/46

72-12   2/46

BLUES BOY
SEE BLUES BOY
    KINGDOM

BLUES BOY
        KINGDOM
101   12/56
(BLUES BOYS)
107   8/57

BLUE SKY
105   4/59

1708   4/59

BOBBIN
101   12/58
103   3/59
106   5/59
109   6/59
111   8/59

BOBBY
5701   6/57

BO-KAY
105   7/59

BOMARC
300   10/58
302   3/59
303   5/59
305   10/59

BONANZA
100   10/55

1925   10/55

BONEY
1004   2/51

BONITA'S
400   10/54

BONNIE
101   6/51

BOP
101   3/57

BOP CAT
101   5/58

BOULDER
105   4/59

BOULEVARD
101   6/59

BOW
SEE ARROW

BOWERY
104   3/55
105   5/55
----
212   3/57
223   1/59
----
301   5/55

1734   12/57

BOWS
.102   4/52
----
105   6/51

BRAD
003   3/58

2210   8/58

BRAMBLE
10	11/51
11	12/51

109	3/57
110	5/57

BRAND
101	4/54

BRAVO
1	9/59

BRAVO
1002	1/49

5509	5/49

BRENT
SEE TIME

BREWSTER
4700	9/52

BRIDGE
21001	9/55

BRITE STAR
763	5/59
764	10/59

BROADCAST
4006	3/48

BROADCAST RECORDING
512	11/50

4071	2/52

BROADWAY
SEE DANA

BRONJO
1000	3/58

BRONZE
126	9/45

BROOKE
102	12/58
106	6/59
109	8/59
110	9/59

BROOK'S
100	6/59

BRUCE
101	12/53
105	2/54
109	7/54
110	10/54
122	12/54
128	3/55

2001	10/54

BRUNSWICK
SEE COLUMBIA
SEE DECCA

BSD
350	8/55

BUCKEYE
222	12/50
224	1/51

BUD
108	5/56

2221	10/56

BUDDHA
1003	4/59

BUDDY
109	10/56
111	7/57
113	8/58
115	1/59
116	7/59

9000	5/56

BUENA VISTA
SEE DISNEYLAND

BULLET
100	4/46
101	5/46
102	1/47
103	9/47
106	6/48
118	11/50
131	3/51
140	12/51

251	4/46
252	5/46
254	10/46
261	11/46
264	3/47
268	4/47
274	5/47
276	7/47
284	4/48
286	8/48
294	10/48
295	11/48
303	3/49
305	6/49
306	7/49
312	9/49
313	10/49
319	11/49
321	12/49
322	1/50
325	6/50
328	9/50
337	10/50
341	5/51

409	10/52

600	4/46
602	6/46
620	11/46
628	1/47
631	3/47
637	4/47
649	3/48
650	4/48
653	5/48
659	8/48
664	9/48
670	10/48

BULLET CON'T
673	4/49
678	7/49
682	8/49
685	9/49
691	10/49
698	11/49
711	4/50
717	6/50
719	8/50
720	11/50
724	12/50
725	1/51
726	2/51
732	3/51
733	4/51
738	6/51
746	1/52
748	5/52

1000	1/47
1001	3/47
1002	7/47
1007	10/47
1011	12/47
1015	2/48
1022	3/48
1036	4/48
1057	6/48
1059	9/48
1064	12/48
1065	3/49
1071	4/49
1076	5/49
1081	7/49
1083	8/49
1084	9/49
1087	12/49
1088	8/50
1089	10/50
1092	11/50
1093	1/51
1097	9/51
1098	12/51
1101	3/52

(DELTA)
202	4/49

(COLLEGIATE)
2950	10/48
2952	12/48
2958	1/49
2965	4/49

(VILLAGE)
500	4/49

BULLSEYE
1	5/55

100	9/55
102	3/56
104	7/56
106	11/56

1001	9/57
1005	3/58
1010	6/58
1014	9/58
1026	5/59
1028	9/59

BURGUNDY
SEE BBS

BURTON
103	5/56

BUZZ
113	4/59
114	5/59

CABOT
104	6/57
105	7/57
108	8/57
109	9/57
110	10/57
111	11/57
120	3/58
126	10/58
127	1/59
130	2/55

CACTUS
121	12/59

1501	7/57

CADENCE
1230	1/53
1231	4/53
1232	8/53

1233	11/53
1235	1/54
1237	3/54
1238	4/54
1241	5/54
1243	7/54
1244	8/54
1246	9/54
1247	10/54
1251	11/54
1255	2/55
1257	3/55
1260	4/55
1262	5/55
1265	6/55
1268	8/55
1272	9/55
1275	10/55
1278	11/55
1280	12/55
1283	1/56
1284	2/56
1287	3/56
1289	4/56
1290	5/56
1293	6/56
1297	7/56
1298	9/56
1300	10/56
1303	11/56
1304	12/56
1305	1/57
1309	3/57
1312	4/57
1324	5/57
1327	7/57
1331	8/57
1333	9/57
1339	11/57
1341	12/57
1342	1/58
1345	2/58
1346	3/58
1348	4/58
1350	7/58
1351	8/58
1352	9/58
1355	10/58
1356	11/58
1358	12/58
1361	1/59
1363	3/59
1365	7/59
1366	8/59
1371	10/59
1372	11/59

CADENCE CON'T	
1376	12/59

1420	10/53
1421	1/54
1422	1/56

1730	1/54
1731	1/56

CADET	
201	4/46

CADILLAC	
101	7/51
103	9/51
105	2/52
118	3/52
120	4/52
123	5/52
140	6/53
146	3/54
150	12/54

CAFAMO	
509	2/50
521	4/50

CAJAM	
275	4/59

CALCORD	
210	7/54

CALECT	
109	9/59

CALICO	
101	11/58
104	1/59
105	4/59
106	5/59
107	7/59
110	10/59

CALVARY	
301	7/52

CALVERT	
100	5/56
102	6/56
104	10/56

CAMARK	
102	6/54
103	10/54

501	6/54
505	7/54

CAMBRIA	
1905	7/57

CAMEO	
5001	5/52

CAMEO	
105	2/57
106	4/57
109	6/57
110	8/57
116	9/57
118	10/57
121	11/57
125	1/58
130	2/58
131	3/58
136	5/58
142	6/58
148	8/58
149	9/58
153	11/58
154	12/58
158	2/59
164	5/59
167	6/59
169	9/59
170	11/59

(PARKWAY)	
801	12/58
804	5/59
808	12/59

CAMM	
132	12/53
134	2/54

CAMMAROTA	
25	5/53
27	10/53
28	11/53

CAMPFIRE	
33	1/58

CAMPUS	
101	3/55
103	5/55
105	8/55
109	5/59
113	9/59

CANADIAN AMERICAN	
102	4/59
103	6/59
106	8/59
107	11/59

5951	2/59

CAN-DEE	
92	8/59

501	9/59
502	11/59

CANDLELIGHT	
1001	6/56
1004	7/56
1005	10/56
1011	4/57
1019	11/57

3067	1/57
3077	4/57

CANDELO	
376	12/58

C & M	
440	8/58

500	5/59

C AND P
104   6/59

CANDY
SEE SIW

CANDY
001   1/59
002   4/59
003   6/59

CANNADY
100   9/59

CANON
502   12/54
510   5/55
511   6/55

CANON
224   3/59

CANTON
211   9/56

CANYON
204   5/53

CAPE
2   3/54

CAPER
1551   8/59

CAPITOL
101   7/42
112   8/42
115   9/42
119   10/42
122   11/42
126   2/43
129   3/43
133   7/43
137   10/43
140   11/43
141   12/43

145	1/44
146	3/44
151	4/44
155	5/44
159	6/44
163	8/44
167	9/44
173	10/44
175	11/44
187	1/45
188	3/45
196	4/45
197	5/45
199	6/45
207	7/45
212	9/45
219	10/45
221	11/45
230	1/46
235	2/46
245	3/46
251	4/46
254	5/46
260	6/46
274	7/46
275	8/46
298	9/46
311	10/46
324	11/46
335	12/46
353	1/47
360	2/47
375	3/47
390	4/47
400	5/47
422	6/47
432	7/47
443	8/47
458	9/47
469	10/47
472	11/47
480	12/47
486	1/48
493	2/48
501	3/48
(ADD PREFIX	
	57-)
544	4/49
590	5/49
665	6/49
683	7/49
704	8/49
720	9/49
759	10/49
774	11/49
785	12/49

818	1/50
868	2/50
891	3/50
960	4/50
1020	5/50
1072	6/50
1091	7/50
1127	8/50
1183	9/50
1244	10/50
1280	11/50
1328	12/50
1349	1/51
1382	2/51
1417	3/51
1468	4/51
1511	5/51
1555	6/51
1594	7/51
1739	8/51
1768	9/51
1807	10/51
1844	11/51
1883	12/51
1918	1/52
1955	2/52
1964	3/52
2036	4/52
2068	5/52
2116	6/52
2143	7/52
2157	7/52
2212	9/52
2250	10/52
2274	11/52
2307	12/52
2317	1/53
2352	2/53
2382	3/53
2420	4/53
2450	5/53
2486	6/53
2514	7/53
2542	8/53
2564	9/53
2594	10/53
2638	11/53
2666	12/53
2698	1/54
2715	2/54
2742	3/54
2770	4/54
2787	5/54
2817	6/54
2853	7/54
2882	8/54

CAPITOL CON'T	
2917	9/54
2919	10/54
2959	11/54
2985	12/54
3010	1/55
3029	2/55
3054	3/55
3085	4/55
3116	5/55
3136	6/55
3171	7/55
3191	8/55
3291	9/55
3244	10/55
3274	11/55
3298	12/55
3310	1/56
3350	2/56
3366	3/56
3405	4/56
3430	5/56
3453	6/56
3485	7/56
3495	8/56
3522	9/56
3565	10/56
3587	11/56
3602	12/56
3613	1/57
3619	2/57
3659	3/57
3706	4/57
3717	5/57
3737	6/57
3752	7/57
3774	8/57
3790	9/57
3820	10/57
3850	11/57
3866	12/57
3874	1/58
3894	2/58
3941	3/58
3961	4/58
3973	5/58
3992	6/58
4011	7/58
4033	8/58
4042	9/58
4074	10/58
4080	11/58
4105	12/58
4114	1/59
4151	2/59
4166	3/59

4178	4/59
4203	5/59
4226	6/59
4244	7/59
4257	8/59
4284	9/59
4287	10/59
4300	11/59
4324	12/59

10021	10/45
10031	11/45
10119	3/48
10163	10/48
10190	2/49

15000	10/47
15015	11/47
15020	12/47
15021	1/48
15032	2/48
15041	3/48
15071	5/48
15119	6/48
15136	7/48
15170	8/48
15199	9/48
15232	10/48
15297	11/48
15316	12/48
15337	1/49
15376	2/49
15407	3/49

20017	4/45
20045	2/46
20053	4/46
20069	11/46

25103	7/48

40000	6/47
40017	7/47
40042	11/47
40069	12/47
40072	1/48
40087	2/48
40092	3/48
40111	4/48
40115	5/48
40122	6/48
40127	7/48
40134	8/48
40137	9/48
40140	10/48
40141	1/49

ADD PREFIX
57-

40151	3/49
40153	4/49
40157	5/49
40174	6/49
40194	7/49
40211	8/49
40227	9/49
40238	10/49
40249	11/49

48001	6/47
48034	3/49

52000	11/48

PREFIX 57-

70000	3/49
70003	4/49
70007	5/49
70013	6/49
70021	7/49
70032	8/49
70037	9/49
70041	10/49
70051	11/49
70057	12/49

71122	7/58
71131	8/58

90063	2/50

(PREP)

100	4/57
104	5/57
105	6/57
111	7/57
113	8/57
115	9/57
118	10/57
121	11/57
125	12/57
128	1/58
136	3/58

CAPRI

777	11/55

CAPRI

2000	7/49

CAPRICE
0050   6/58
0056   4/58

CAPROCK
100   12/57
102   3/58
104   9/58
108   2/59
113   7/59
114   9/59

CARAVAN
18   2/500
----
301   4/50

CARAVAN
15605   7/56

15701   2/57

CARDILL
1   10/54

CARDHILL
3068   1/55

52026   1/55

CARDINAL
25001   1/47

CARDINAL
1002   9/52
1005   11/52
1006   3/53
1012   10/53
1015   2/54
1016   6/54
1023   8/54
1025   11/54
1031   3/55
1037   5/55
1038   7/55
1044   8/55
1045   10/55
1048   11/55
1049   2/56

1050   5/56

5002   1/55

CARL SOBIE
2333   8/49

CARLTON
450   1/58
452   2/58
453   3/58
457   4/58
463   5/58
467   6/58
472   7/58
473   8/58
483   9/58
484   10/58
485   11/58
490   12/58
497   1/59
500   2/59
504   3/58
509   4/59
512   5/59
514   6/59
516   7/59
517   8/59
518   9/59
521   10/59
522   11/59

(GUARANTEED)
200   8/59
201   9/59
202   10/59
203   11/59
204   12/59

CARNATION
101   12/57
----
501   9/53

CARNIVAL
505   5/50
----
705   3/50

3000A   2/55

5006   5/51

CAROL
100   4/59

CAROLINA
1001   4/53

CAROLYN
100   3/52

CAROUSEL
44   12/58
----
66   12/58
----
100   2/57

2002   5/51
2006   10/51
2007   12/51

CARROL
5001   2/49
5004   3/49

CARROLLTON
800   5/59

CARTER
1001   11/57

CARTHAY
101   4/59
102   6/59

CASA GRANDE
113   11/54

4031   4/54
4036   9/56
4037   6/57
4038   12/57
4039   6/58

CASCADE
003   11/57

5901   2/59

CASCADE CON'T
5903   3/59
5906   4/59
5908   5/59
5909   6/59
5912   9/59

CASH
SEE MONEY

CASHMERE
1001   3/59

CASINO
129   7/55
----
170   3/56

CASINO
SEE ROULETTE

CASTLE
500   3/48
502   5/48
512   12/48
518   9/49

1103   4/49
1139   7/49

1252   4/48
1255   7/48
1257   9/48
1258   4/49
1281   11/49

1315   6/49

1401   6/49
1405   7/49

1515   7/49

1601   4/50

(BRENT)
7000   5/59
7003   8/59
7005   9/59
7006   10/59
7007   11/59

(JADE)
106   5/57
----
201   12/50
(JAX)
101   6/58
103   2/59
----
314   8/53

1000   10/59

4004   12/59

(HARLEM)
2331   4/55
2333   5/55
2336   6/55

(SHAD)
102   4/55

5001   11/58
5003   12/58
5005   2/59
5007   6/59
5008   7/59
5012   10/59
5013   11/59

(SITTIN'-IN)
503   9/48
508   10/48
509   11/48
512   1/49
514   4/49

2000   9/48

16000   9/48

18000   10/48
(SITTIN'-IN
          WITH)
543   2/50
550   4/50
583   11/50
584   12/50
599   5/51
607   7/51
608   8/51
612   9/51
621   12/51

(TIME)
3   11/58

100   5/57
101   7/57
102   9/57

1004   1/59
1006   2/59
1008   3/59
1011   5/59
1012   6/59
1013   7/59
1014   8/59
1016   9/59
1017   11/59

6600   6/58
6602   8/58

CASTLE
502   9/58
503   11/58
505   3/59
506   6/59
507   8/59

CAT
SEE ATLANTIC

CATALINA
4514   4/59

CAVALCADE
4764   5/57

CAVALIER
501   11/56
----
805   9/51
813   9/52
818   12/52
825   5/53
828   12/53
832   4/54
834   8/54
836   9/54
842   2/55
846   3/55
850   5/55
852   7/55
859   5/56
869   11/56
873   4/57

CAVALIER CON'T
876   4/58
879   3/59
880   9/59

CAVE
444   8/57

CAVERN
101   6/59

CAWTHORNE
505   6/59

CELEBRITY
SEE BEACON

CELESTIAL
108   1/58
114   6/58

CELTIC
1039   1/51

CENTAUR
852   12/59

CENTER
SEE DERBY
PAGE 157

CENTRAL
51   12/51

CENTRAL
2600   7/57
2602   7/58
2605   11/58

CENTRAL
SEE DERBY
PAGE 157

CENTURY
102   3/54
105   8/54

107   9/54
108   11/54
----
710   3/55
711   4/55

CENTURY
1501   8/49
1505   12/49

3002   8/46
3014   5/47

4006   2/48
4158   6/58

CHA CHA
701   7/59

CHALLANGE
1002   1/50

CHALLANGE
1001   4/57
1002   6/57
1007   9/57
1008   10/57
1013   12/57
1014   1/58

59000   3/58
59003   4/58
59007   5/58
59010   6/58
59016   7/58
59019   8/58
59022   9/58
59027   10/58
59028   11/58
59036   2/59
59039   3/59
59044   4/59
59045   5/59
59049   6/59
59053   8/59
59055   10/59
59058   11/59
59062   12/59

(REPUBLIC)
2001   11/59

(JACKPOT)
48000   5/58
48001   7/58
48007   8/58
48009   9/58
48012   10/58
48013   12/58
48015   2/59
48017   4/59
48018   6/59
48020   9/59

CHAM
001   7/58

CHAMP
102   9/58

CHAMPION
SEE SPECIALTY

CHAMPION
1001   12/58
1015   8/59

CHANCE
1101   3/51
1114   5/52
1116   6/52
1117   8/52
1123   11/52
1128   1/53
1129   2/53
1133   3/53
1134   5/53
1138   6/53
1140   7/53
1142   8/53
1143   9/53
1144   10/53
1150   11/53
1151   1/54
1153   4/54
1155   5/54
1156   6/54
1157   8/54
1161   10/54
1162   11/54

3000   6/53
3002   7/53

CHANCE CON'T
3006	1/54
3009	2/54
3014	3/54

5000	4/52
5001	6/52
5002	11/52
5007	10/53
(SABRE)	
101	8/53
102	9/53
104	11/53
105	2/54
109	8/54

CHANCELLOR
1000	3/57
1001	4/57
1003	5/57
1005	8/57
1006	9/57
1007	10/57
1008	11/57
1011	1/58
1015	2/58
1016	3/58
1017	4/58
1018	6/58
1022	7/58
1023	8/58
1024	9/58
1028	11/58
1029	12/58
1031	2/59
1032	3/59
1036	5/59
1037	6/59
1040	8/59
1043	10/59
1045	11/59

CHANSON
1000	12/59

CHARLES
7-11	12/52
712	5/54

CHARM
101	9/59

CHARM
1003	7/48

CHART
601	8/55
602	9/55
604	10/55
608	12/55
609	2/56
611	3/56
618	5/56
619	6/56
633	11/56
634	1/57

10001	12/59

CHASE
1643	2/57

2600	11/56

CHATEAU
2001	6/55

CHECKER
SEE ARISTOCRAT

CHECKERED
7001	11/46

CHELSEA
533	10/59

CHEROKEE
500	4/59
502	6/59
503	9/59

980	11/58
1019	12/59

CHERRY
1002	7/59
1008	11/59

CHERYL ANN
3109	3/57

CHESS
SEE ARISTOCRAT

CHESTERFIELD
348	8/54
352	12/54

CHEYANNE
108	7/59

CHIC
1001	9/56
1004	11/56
1006	2/57
1007	4/57
1010	5/57
1013	7/57
1014	9/57

CHICAGO
237	10/57

CHICAGO
SEE SOUTHERN

CHIEF
6368	5/46

CHIEF
7000	4/57
7001	5/57
7002	6/57
7005	11/57
7006	12/57
7010	6/58

CHIRP
5901	12/59

CHOCK
103	5/58
104	6/58
105	8/58

CHOCK CON'T
109   11/58

CHOICE
845   4/56
846   5/56
848   6/56
850   4/57
851   5/57
856   1/58

CHOLLY
7089   3/58

CHORD
125   2/48
----
151   4/48
----
201   12/47
----
640   9/47
664   2/48

CHORD
1305   3/59

CHRISTIAN
           FAITH
825   2/54

CHRISTY
101   12/57
102   1/58
106   11/58
107   2/59
108   8/59
110   8/59
115   10/59

CIMMARON
2767   12/58

4041   6/59
4042   9/59

4283   6/57

CINDY
1   12/55
2   3/56

3009   8/58

CIRCLE
45   4/57
----
101   4/59
----
282   5/59

CIRCLE
3005

CI-SUM
1154   2/55

11576   2/56

CITATION
146   4/51

1154   12/51
1160   1/52
1167   5/52
1168   7/52

CITATION
1030   4/58
1032   5/58
1035   12/58
1038   3/59
1039   6/59
1042   8/59

C.J.
605   5/59

6038   9/59

CLARION
101   8/49

CLARO
5852   10/58

5911   2/59
5914   12/59

CLASS
SEE EXCELSIOR

CLASSIC
1000   12/57

CLEF
101   2/48

CLEF
89082   11/53
89086   12/53
89090   1/54
89097   2/54
89101   3/54
89106   4/54
89113   5/54
89114   6/54
89118   7/54
89126   1/55
89149   6/55
89150   8/55
89166   3/56
89170   5/56
89171   7/56
89172   12/56

(NORGRAN)
100   5/54
105   6/54
108   7/54
120   8/54
128   1/55
142   6/55
143   7/55
146   12/55
148   1/56
149   5/56
151   8/56

(VERVE)
2000   2/56
2005   3/56
2007   6/56
2013   6/56
2014   7/56
2019   9/56
2023   10/56
2027   11/56

CLEF CON'T
  (VERVE) CON'T
2028   12/56
2030   2/57
2031   3/57
2042   4/57
2048   5/57
2058   6/57

10064   7/57
10127   4/58
10128   5/58
10140   6/58
10141   7/58
10152   10/58
10154   11/58
19155   12/58
10161   1/59
10162   2/59
10166   3/59
10169   3/59
10174   6/59
10176   7/59
10181   9/59
10190   10/59

89173   7/57
89186   8/58
89187   11/58
89188   4/59

CLEFF-TONE
157   4/59

1004   11/58

CLEO
531   5/53

CLICK
103   11/47
115   12/48
----
326   12/49

CLIFF
102   7/57

CLIMAX
101   3/59

---

102   6/59
104   8/59
105   10/59
106   11/59

CLIPPER
1001   4/50
1002   5/50
1009   2/51
1010   6/51

CLOCK
1006   9/58
1007   12/58
1009   2/59
1010   4/59
1011   5/59
1014   9/59

CLOUD
1019   2/53

CLOVER
701   4/48
703   5/48
----
777   5/48

CLUB
1012   12/56

9035   7/59

CLUB '51
101   5/55

CLYMAX
2   6/58
----
103   5/59

C M I
1001   5/58

COAST
101   7/45

---

501   6/45
----
701   6/47

2005   6/45
2007   8/45
2008   9/45
2012   10/45
2013   11/45
2018   2/46
2022   3/46
223   5/46
226   6/46
230   7/46
234   8/46
235   9/46
239   11/46
242   1/47
249   2/47
253   3/47
256   5/47
261   6/47
262   7/47
266   1/48
269   4/48

8004   1/47
8007   4/47
8026   12/47
8036   2/48
8048   4/48
8053   7/48
8062   10/48

9001   5/48

(PEERLESS)
2358   1/47

COBRA
300   9/49

COBRA
1001   2/57

5000   9/56
5004   12/56
5007   2/57
5010   4/57
5012   5/57
5013   6/57

CO CO
152   11/58

CODA
511   12/45

8000   6/49

CODE
711   7/58

CO-ED
SEE
    FRATERNITY

COED
SEE
    FRATERNITY

COIN
101   7/56

1502   8/49

COLE
100   9/59

COLEMAN
100   1/49

5963   1/48
5971   3/48
5978   5/48
5989   7/48
5997   12/48
6002   2/49
6009   6/49

COLLECTOR'S
CLASSICS
1001   5/54

COLLECTOR'S
ITEMS
805   3/46

COLLEGIATE
SEE BULLET

COLLEGIATE
400   2/59

COLONIAL
401   4/55
405   7/55
415   7/56
420   9/56
430   2/57
433   5/57
435   8/57
----
721   11/57

7002   7/59
7003   8/59
7004   11/59

7777   6/58

8888   11/58

9999   11/58

COLONY
SEE IMPERIAL

COLPIX
104   12/58
105   2/59
112   4/59
124   8/59
125   9/59

COLT
103   5/59

COLT "45"
1009   5/59

COLUMBIA
20428   5/48
20441   6/48
20457   7/48
20463   8/48
20476   9/48
20493   10/48
20508   11/48
20511   12/48
20535   1/49

20546   2/49
20552   3/49
20562   4/49
20590   6/49
20591   7/49
20598   8/49
20625   10/49
20633   11/49
20644   12/49
20656   1/50
20674   3/50
20680   4/50
20702   5/50
20709   6/50
20710   7/50
20730   8/50
20739   9/50
20755   10/50
20772   1/51
20784   2/51
20793   3/51
20798   4/51
20800   5/51
20814   6/51
20822   7/51
20842   8/51
20855   9/51
20862   10/51
20866   11/51
20883   12/51
20894   3/52
20934   4/52
20948   6/52
20972   7/52
20994   8/52
21006   9/52
21020   10/52
21032   11/52
21048   12/52
21061   1/53
21076   3/53
21089   4/53
21108   5/53
21120   6/53
21132   7/53
21142   8/53
21157   9/53
21166   10/53
21186   11/53
21197   1/54
21208   2/54
21226   3/54
21227   4/54
21237   5/54
21256   6/54
21266   8/54

COLUMBIA CON'T					
21299	9/54	35457	6/40	36883	11/45
21313	10/54	35563	7/40	36902	12/45
21322	11/54	35596	8/40	36910	1/46
21335	12/54	35713	9/40	36932	2/46
21339	1/55	35742	10/40	36950	3/46
21352	2/55	35868	1/41	36976	4/46
21361	3/55	35923	2/41	36991	5/46
21379	4/55	35977	3/41	36992	6/46
21392	5/55	36023	4/41	37050	7/46
21404	6/55	36081	5/41	37074	8/46
21413	7/55	36150	6/41	37078	9/46
21429	8/55	36209	7/41	37093	10/46
21439	9/55	36255	8/41	37146	11/46
21449	10/55	36306	9/41	37194	12/46
21462	11/55	36389	10/41	37216	1/47
21471	12/55	36403	11/41	37235	2/47
21480	1/56	36444	12/41	37262	3/47
21498	2/56	36468	1/42	37330	4/47
21504	3/56	36514	2/42	37344	5/47
21510	4/56	36524	3/42	37385	6/47
21515	5/56	36550	4/42	37486	7/47
21522	6/56	36565	5/42	37591	8/47
21531	7/56	36598	6/42	37875	9/47
21537	8/56	36609	7/42	37940	10/47
21550	9/56	36617	8/42	37951	11/47
21560	10/56	36640	9/42	37954	12/47
21569	11/56	36644	10/42	38056	1/48
---------		36658	11/42	38070	2/48
30120	6/48	36668	1/43	38108	3/48
30127	7/48	36670	2/43	38151	4/48
30134	8/48	36673	3/43	38178	5/48
30140	9/48	36675	4/43	38216	6/48
30141	10/48	36676	5/43	38267	7/48
30144	11/48	36678	7/43	38274	8/48
30148	12/48	36679	9/43	38297	9/48
30149	1/49	36683	11/43	38314	10/48
30152	2/49	36684	1/44	38334	11/48
30154	3/49	36691	3/44	38371	12/48
30159	5/49	36698	4/44	38386	1/49
30161	6/49	36712	5/44	38413	2/49
30164	7/49	36718	6/44	38417	3/49
30169	8/49	36724	7/44	38453	4/49
30172	9/49	36731	8/44	38464	5/49
30174	11/49	36737	9/44	38504	6/49
30179	1/50	36753	10/44	38521	7/49
30196	3/50	36754	12/44	38555	8/49
30198	4/50	36764	1/45	38586	10/49
30204	5/50	36774	2/45	38622	11/49
30208	7/50	36785	3/45	38642	12/49
30218	8/50	36795	4/45	38677	1/50
30221	9/50	36805	5/45	38708	2/50
30223	11/50	36816	6/45	38721	3/50
30239	5/51	36836	7/45	38751	4/50
---------		36840	8/45	38783	5/50
		36850	9/45	38838	6/50
35393	4/40	36872	10/45	38885	7/50

COLUMBIA CON'T	
38904	8/50
38929	9/50
38990	10/50
39026	11/50
39067	12/50
39142	1/51
39185	2/51
39217	3/51
39248	4/51
39330	5/51
39416	6/51
39446	7/51
39490	8/51
39533	9/51
39595	10/51
39602	11/51
39604	12/51
39633	1/52
39639	2/52
39697	3/52
39726	4/52
39767	6/52
39788	7/52
39817	8/52
39856	9/52
39879	10/52
39889	11/52
39906	12/52
39912	1/53
39938	2/53
39968	3/53
39970	4/53
40003	5/53
40006	6/53
40023	7/53
40040	8/53
40064	9/53
40088	10/53
40121	11/53
40144	12/53
40152	1/54
40156	2/54
40205	3/54
40208	4/54
40224	5/54
40267	7/54
40291	8/54
40311	9/54
40328	10/54
40361	11/54
40389	12/54
40406	1/55
40434	2/55
40451	3/55
40487	4/55

40498	5/55
40517	6/55
40537	7/55
40550	8/55
40561	9/55
40568	10/55
40596	11/55
40611	12/55
40636	1/56
40659	2/56
40674	3/56
40689	4/56
40700	5/56
40704	6/56
40716	7/56
40737	8/56
40746	9/56
40772	10/56
40779	11/56
40794	12/56
40827	2/57
40849	3/57
40884	4/57
40909	5/57
40940	6/57
40956	7/57
40981	8/57
41000	9/57
41012	10/57
41021	11/57
41068	12/57
41090	1/58
41113	2/58
41133	3/58
41157	4/58
41167	5/58
41194	6/58
41201	7/58
41221	8/58
41238	9/58
41281	10/58
41291	11/58
41304	12/58
41325	2/59
41355	3/59
41371	4/59
41392	5/59
41411	6/59
41423	7/59
41438	8/59
41470	9/59
41497	10/59
41511	11/59
41539	12/59

(BRUNSWICK)	
6205	3/43

8440	1/40

(HARMONY)	
1007	7/49
1067	8/49
1069	10/49
1083	11/49

(ALPINE)	
50	8/59
51	9/59
54	12/59

(EPIC)	
9001	11/53
9006	12/53
9013	1/54
9017	2/54
9027	3/54
9029	4/54
9040	5/54
9055	6/54
9060	7/54
9063	8/54
9068	9/54
9075	10/54
9077	11/54
9089	12/54
9090	1/55
9091	2/55
9097	3/55
9099	4/55
9103	5/55
9106	6/55
9110	7/55
9114	8/55
9117	9/55
9123	10/55
9132	11/55
9134	12/55
9140	1/56
9145	2/56
9153	3/56
9162	4/56
9165	5/56
9169	6/56
9174	7/56
9176	8/56
9180	9/56
9187	10/56
9190	11/56
9195	12/56

COLUMBIA CON'T					
(EPIC)		6278	8/41	6986	7/53
9197	1/57	6320	9/41	6988	8/53
9199	2/57	6391	10/41	7013	11/53
9204	3/57	6429	11/41	7015	12/53
9213	5/57	6476	12/41	7016	1/54
9219	6/57	6518	1/42	7018	2/54
9227	7/57	6571	2/42	7022	4/54
9228	8/57	6604	3/42	7029	5/54
9232	9/57	6636	4/42	7031	6/54
9233	10/57	6654	5/42	7034	7/54
9247	11/57	6693	10/42	7037	8/54
9257	12/57	6697	11/42	7041	9/54
9260	1/58	6701	12/42	7042	10/54
9262	2/58	6702	1/43	7047	11/54
9264	3/58	6708	3/43	7048	12/54
9268	4/58	6713	6/43	7050	2/55
9273	5/58	6715	9/43	7053	4/55
9276	6/58	6716	2/44	7055	5/55
9278	7/58	6718	3/44	7056	6/55
9282	8/58	6719	5/44	7057	7/55
9288	10/58	6720	7/44	7060	9/55
9296	11/58	6723	9/44	7062	10/55
9299	12/58	6725	10/44	7064	12/55
9300	1/59	6726	11/44	7065	1/56
9303	2/59	6728	12/44	7067	2/56
9307	3/59	6732	1/45	7068	10/56
9308	4/59	6733	2/45	7072	11/56
9311	5/59	6735	3/45	7074	12/56
9320	6/59	6739	4/45	7077	1/57
9325	7/59	6741	5/45	7082	3/57
9328	8/59	6743	6/45	7084	4/57
9331	9/59	6745	7/45	7086	6/57
9340	10/59	6747	8/45	7088	7/57
9344	11/59	---------		7089	8/57
9352	12/59	6800	6/51	7091	9/57
---------		6808	8/51	7094	11/57
(VOCALION)		6814	9/51	7096	12/57
5405	3/40	6828	10/51	7098	2/58
5443	4/40	6835	11/51	7099	3/58
5491	5/40	6841	12/51	7100	4/58
5540	6/40	6851	2/52	7102	5/58
5552	7/40	6863	3/52	7103	7/58
BECOMES OKEH		6865	4/52	7104	8/58
---------		6882	5/52	7107	11/58
(OKEH)		6883	6/52	7108	1/59
5627	7/40	6892	7/52	7110	2/59
5701	8/40	6898	8/52	7112	3/59
5779	9/40	6907	9/52	7114	4/59
5968	1/41	6915	10/52	7117	5/59
5992	2/41	6925	11/52	7119	6/59
6053	3/41	6935	1/53	7120	7/59
6098	4/41	6938	2/53	7121	8/59
6133	5/41	6949	3/53	7122	9/59
6201	6/41	6951	4/53	7124	10/59
6257	7/41	6957	5/53		
		6978	6/53		

COLUMBIA
  GRAPHOPHONE
3500   9/49

COLUMBINE
101   2/50
106   3/50
108   5/50
109   9/50
110   10/50
113   11/50

COMBO
1   12/51
55   4/54
64   1/55
113 4/56
155 8/59

COMET
SEE BLACK AND
        WHITE

COMET
101   8/57
102   12/57
103   4/58
104   4/59

COMET
5201   4/52

COMMAND
4008   12/59

COMMAND
5006   12/49

COMMODORE
526   3/40
546   5/44
553   7/44
554   11/44
557   2/45
559   5/45
562   6/45
568   12/45
570   6/46

574   8/46
575   11/46
580   4/47
586   7/47
595   9/47
602   10/47
618   7/48

1511   5/44
1515   6/44
1518   12/44
1519   12/48

3005   10/47

7500   12/47
7504   3/48
7506   8/48
7549   1/49
7552   4/49
7557   11/49
7558   11/49

10000   2/52

COMMAND
17   8/50

5010   2/50
5015   3/50
5020   4/50

CONCEPT
897   5/57
900   4/58

1001   9/58

CONGRESS
111   12/58

CONQUEST
1001   7/58

CONSTELLATION
4013   5/46

CONTEMPORARY
353   6/53
356   9/53

358   12/53
361   10/56
368   4/59

CONTENDER
1313   7/58
1317   4/59

CONTINENTAL
115   10/49
----
802   1/50
816   6/52

1139   2/44
1141   3/44
1142   4/44
1144   6/44
1149   7/44
1154   11/44
1155   12/44
1161   7/45
1163   10/45
1166   11/45
1171   1/46
1175   4/46
1188   8/46
1221   1/48
1242   7/48
1251   11/48
1264   6/49
1267   8/49
1271   5/50

3000   4/42
3016   7/44
3017   8/44

5009   5/44
5017   9/44
5018   10/44
5021   11/44
5031   12/44
5040   10/45
5050   1/46

5103   2/47

6000   6/45
6007   11/45
6015   1/46
6031   1/47
6038   2/47
6039   4/47

CONTINENTAL
CON'T
6053	5/47
6059	9/47
6065	5/48
6066	7/48
6070	10/48

8009	2/47
8021	3/47
8023	4/47
8030	9/47
8036	5/48
8038	3/49
8041	4/49
8044	8/49
8046	10/49
8053	3/50
8055	5/50

10000	10/45
10002	1/46
10008	7/47

11001	1/47
11005	1/49

15073	3/47

COOK
4407	9/59

31851	9/59

COOL
106	7/58
111	12/58
115	1/59

CO-OP
1501	8/57
1503	9/57
1504	11/57

CORAL
SEE DECCA

CORBEN
675	4/50

CORBIN
734	8/56

CORDON
1227	4/57

CORMAC
1052	1/50
1091	2/50
1094	4/50
1146	11/50
1160	12/50
1168	2/51
1175	4/51
1193	8/51
1196	10/51

CORNEL
3001	2/58

CORONA
101	4/50
102	6/50

1000	7/53
1005	5/55

CORONATION
101	6/56
102	8/56
103	2/57
104	8/57
105	3/58

1000	5/59

CORONET
1	3/46

100	4/47

500	3/50
503	7/50

5001	4/52

CORONET
101	11/54

CORONET
1303	4/59

CORSICAN
0058	5/59

CORT
1314	11/58

CORVET
1011	2/58

CORVETTE
1000	6/58
1001	7/58
1004	9/58
1005	11/58
1008	12/58
1009	4/59

COSMIC
104	1/58

1001	8/56

COSMO
COSMOPOLITAN
451	7/45
470	1/46
473	4/46
478	5/46
484	6/46
499	7/46
502	8/46
584	9/47

COTILLION
5-0005	11/50

COTILLION
2532	9/55

COUNTERPOINT
008	9/58
010	1/59
011	3/59

COUNTERPOINT
CON'T
451   9/57

10-013   4/59

COUNTRY
1   6/59

COUNTRY
           JUBILEE
517   6/59
519   9/59
523   10/59

COVER
5941   5/59
5971   8/59
5981   9/59

COVERED
           WAGON
100   6/49

COWBOY
101   9/46
105   10/49
----
202   12/46
204   3/48
----
302   11/47
----
402   12/47
----
501   9/47
502   6/48
----
601   6/48
----
701   6/48
----
801   7/48
802   12/48
----
901   9/48

1101   9/48

1201   8/48
1202   3/49

1301   12/48

1501   10/49

1701   11/50

COWTOWN
           HOEDOWN
777   6/57
778   7/57

CO-WEST
501   7/59

COXX
588   1/57

COZY
110   2/48
130   3/48
149   2/49
----
206   7/49
254   9/50
331   4/52
386   7/52

1001   12/46
1005   1/47

41010   12/46

CRAFT
111   5/59
116   8/59

CRAZY
1002   5/55

CREATIVE
           ARTISTS
202   7/55
203   10/55

CRECENT
1001   3/55

CRESCENDO
116   7/52
118   9/52
120   10/52
126   11/52

CREST
100   10/56
----
511   5/59

1006   10/55
1009   2/56
1011   4/56
1014   5/56
1023   7/56
1027   8/56
1030   10/56
1038   3/58
1040   4/58
1042   5/58
1047   6/58
1050   8/58
1052   10/58
1054   12/58
1057   3/59
1059   4/59
1060   5/59
1061   6/59
1063   8/59
1065   10/59
1067   11/59

CRITERIAN
103   10/55

CROSLEY
103   5/53
106   6/53

CROSLEY
202   2/59
216   9/59

CROSS COUNTRY
100   3/59
101   5/59
----
504   1/55
506   5/55
512   10/55

CROSS COUNTRY
CON'T
518   1/56

CROSSDALE
207   8/48

CROWN
SEE MODERN

CROWN
100   2/46
148   8/47
154   10/47
156   11/47

CROWN
1101   5/52
- - - - - - - - -
3588   6/53

CRYSTAL
167   7/48
174   10/48
187   1/49
211   4/49
225   11/49
249   12/49
256   5/50
279   7/50
289   8/50
291   9/50
302   11/50
330   5/51
373   4/53
405   8/53
448   12/53
- - - - - - - - -
640   5/50
- - - - - - - - -
1003   12/47

CRYSTAL
108   4/59
- - - - - - - - -
501   2/58
503   5/58

CRYSTALETTE
353   6/53
- - - - - - - - -
605   7/47
608   8/49
611   10/49
612   11/49
616   2/50
626   3/50
628   7/50
643   11/50
647   12/50
649   4/53
652   5/53
659   11/53
662   12/53
665   1/54
701   5/56
703   7/56
706   9/56
707   11/56
708   2/57
709   3/57
712   5/57
714   9/57
715   12/57
717   3/58
719   9/58
724   1/59
725   3/59
727   4/59
728   5/59
730   6/59
732   8/59
734   10/59
- - - - - - - - -
1202   4/49

CRYSTAL TONE
504   12/47
513   2/48
520   4/48
521   6/48
- - - - - - - - -
1001   12/47

CUB
SEE MGM

CUE
818   1/59
- - - - - - - - -
1200   5/58

1212   9/58
- - - - - - - - -
7923   12/55
7926   3/56
7928   5/56
7934   3/57

CULLMAN
6402   5/58
6403   9/58
6404   10/58
6405   12/58
6408   1/59
6409   3/59
6412   4/59
6415   5/59

CUPID
100   9/59
- - - - - - - - -
1001   6/58
- - - - - - - - -
1212   12/59

CURTIS
256   11/58

CUSTOM
101   7/52

CUSTOM SOUND
STUDIO
201   11/53
202   12/53

CYCLE
101   3/55

CYCLONE
107   6/47
- - - - - - - - -
606   5/47
608   7/47

CYMBOL
25001   6/55
25002   11/55

D

1000	5/58
1004	6/58
1005	7/58
1009	8/58
1013	9/58
1017	10/58
1023	11/58
1026	12/58
1033	1/59
1037	2/59
1043	3/59
1051	4/59
1057	5/59
1062	6/59
1072	7/59
1078	8/59
1086	9/59
1096	10/59
1100	11/59
1103	12/59

D

12054	4/51

DAB

101	3/59

DADE

1804	12/59

DAFFAN

102	3/56
103	4/56
104	5/56
106	9/56
108	12/56
110	3/57
112	4/57
116	11/59

DAJA

501	4/58
504	2/59

DALE

100	3/57
102	7/57
104	4/58
105	5/58
106	7/58
107	10/58
109	11/58
110	2/59
111	4/59
112	6/59
113	8/59
114	10/59

1004	5/58
1016	11/58

26378	6/57

DAMON

11133	1/48
11135	9/48

11216	2/49
11221	4/49
11229	11/49

12066	10/53

DA-MAR

2001	8/59

DAMCO

101	9/58

DANA

629	4/53

2101	11/52
2106	7/53
2114	12/56
2115	5/57
2126	3/58
2129	4/59
2130	7/59

3124	6/53
3192	2/55
3240	3/57
3269	9/57
(BROADWAY)	
101	2/52

1003	3/51
1004	5/51
1008	8/51

DANCE-TONE

302	4/49
323	5/49
340	7/49
353	8/49
363	9/49

1133	6/49
1136	8/49
1137	9/49
1139	10/39

D & C

500	10/59

D AND D

45-1903	8/48

D & L

0020	8/57

DANGOLD

2001	4/59

DARLING

2121	6/52

DART

100	6/59
104	7/59
109	9/59
125	12/59

301	9/59

404	11/59

1114	3/59

DART

2000	10/49

7001	1/50
7004	2/50

DASH

777	3/56

DASH CON'T
55001   3/58

DATE
1001   2/58
1003   4/58
1005   6/58
1006   7/58

DAUPHIN
103   9/59

DAVIS
SEE BEACON

DAWN
201   1/54
206   4/54
207   6/54
210   11/54
212   2/55
213   5/55
214   11/55
216   5/56
217   8/56
219   9/56
220   11/56
223   12/56
224   2/57
228   5/57
229   6/57
233   8/57
235   3/58
236   6/58

DAY-Z-BEL
101   2/58
----
711   10/58
713   11/59

DBC
1232   6/59

D C
94-78   6/53
----
228   12/55
----

400   5/56

0409   11/57
0412   2/59
0416   3/59
0417   4/59
0420   6/59
0421   8/59

1200   10/48

4102   10/48
4106   11/48
4107   12/48
4114   5/49

8023   6/47
8024   10/47
8028   11/47
8030   12/47
8042   1/48
8047   2/48
8048   5/48
8052   6/48
8056   7/48
8057   11/48
8058   4/49
8059   10/49

DDR
102   2/53

DEB
232   2/59
----
500   10/58
506   2/59
508   3/59
----
781   6/59

1001   10/56
1002   5/57
1008   12/58

DEBBIE
101   9/58
102   11/58

1408   5/59

DE'BESTH
116   7/58

1111   2/58
1117   4/59

DEBUT
111   11/54

DECANTER
2   11/58
----
101   9/58
103   2/59
104   7/59

DECATUR
1003   10/51
1005   7/52
1007   5/53

2001   10/51

DECCA
2236   1/40
2400   8/40

2925   1/40
2961   2/40
2997   3/40
3065   4/40
3097   5/40
3161   6/40
3247   7/40
3272   8/40
3346   9/40
3375   10/40
3420   11/40
3478   12/40
3560   1/41
3590   2/41
3675   4/41
3715   5/41
3810   6/41
3856   7/41
3889   8/41
3968   9/41
4021   10/41
4030   11/41
4094   12/41
4107   1/42
4167   3/42

DECCA CON'T					
4270	4/42	6111	8/45	18672	5/45
4309	5/42	6112	10/45	18684	6/45
4340	8/42	---------		18692	7/45
4356	9/42	8507	4/41	18698	8/45
4375	10/42	8552	6/41	18703	9/45
4395	11/42	8559	7/41	18715	10/45
4396	12/42	8560	10/41	18725	11/45
4400	2/43	8570	11/41	18739	12/45
4403	3/43	8583	12/41	18764	2/46
4415	5/43	8593	1/42	18800	3/46
4418	6/43	8638	11/42	18830	4/46
4420	7/43	8646	12/42	18873	5/46
4425	10/43	8647	1/43	18911	7/46
4426	11/43	8648	2/43	18923	11/46
4428	1/44	8650	3/43	---------	
4434	2/44	8653	9/43	23277	10/43
4435	3/44	8654	12/43	23281	11/43
4438	4/44	8657	3/44	23297	3/44
4440	5/44	8659	4/44	23300	4/44
4443	6/44	8660	7/44	23319	5/44
4446	7/44	8661	10/44	23340	6/44
4447	8/44	8662	11/44	23344	7/44
4448	10/44	8668	1/45	23348	8/44
4449	11/44	8669	2/45	23350	9/44
4454	4/45	---------		23355	10/44
---------		18353	5/42	23356	11/44
5874	11/40	18360	6/42	23367	12/44
5901	12/40	18393	7/42	23377	1/45
5933	5/41	18429	8/42	23383	2/45
5937	6/41	18472	9/42	23397	3/45
5958	9/41	18482	10/42	23403	4/45
5976	10/41	18524	11/42	23423	5/45
5991	11/41	18541	1/43	23428	6/45
5993	12/41	18542	4/43	23436	7/45
6003	1/42	18545	5/43	23444	8/45
6023	3/42	18548	7/43	23456	9/45
6030	4/42	18561	9/43	23467	11/45
6037	5/42	18564	10/43	23473	12/45
6050	6/42	18567	11/43	23478	2/46
6056	7/42	18570	12/43	23524	3/46
6058	8/42	18573	1/44	23532	4/46
6063	9/42	18583	2/44	23554	5/46
6068	10/42	18591	3/44	23563	6/46
6074	11/42	18595	4/44	23600	8/46
6079	2/43	18598	5/44	23656	9/46
6083	3/43	18606	6/44	23670	10/46
6091	10/43	18609	7/44	23713	11/46
6095	3/44	18615	8/44	23758	12/46
6097	4/44	18617	9/44	23770	1/47
6100	7/44	18623	10/44	23804	2/47
6103	10/44	18627	11/44	23817	3/47
6105	1/45	18637	12/44	23852	4/47
6106	2/45	18639	1/45	23903	5/47
6107	3/45	18649	2/45	23946	6/47
6109	6/45	18657	3/45	23976	7/47
		18665	4/45	24103	8/47

DECCA CON'T		27397	1/51	29755	12/55
24173	9/47	27415	2/51	29806	2/56
24195	10/47	27454	3/51	29820	3/56
24258	11/47	27516	4/51	29889	4/56
24259	12/47	27603	6/51	29950	5/56
24283	1/48	27640	7/51	29974	6/56
24309	2/48	27681	8/51	29994	7/56
24375	3/48	27748	9/51	30039	8/56
24403	4/48	27792	10/51	30050	9/56
24409	5/48	27834	11/51	30097	10/56
24441	6/48	27880	12/51	30123	11/56
24469	7/48	27946	1/52	30144	12/56
24480	8/48	27953	2/52	30198	1/57
24495	9/48	28030	3/52	30221	2/57
24506	10/48	28074	4/52	30242	3/57
24508	11/48	28216	5/52	30279	4/57
24530	12/48	28224	6/52	30319	5/57
24531	1/49	28288	7/52	30345	6/57
24550	2/49	28328	8/52	30383	7/57
24594	3/49	28385	9/52	30406	8/57
24622	4/49	28421	10/52	30436	9/57
24629	5/49	28442	11/52	30454	10/57
24639	6/49	28494	12/52	30503	11/57
24671	7/49	28554	1/53	30521	12/57
24699	8/49	28575	2/53	30543	1/58
24720	9/49	28610	3/53	30575	2/58
24768	10/49	28646	4/53	30592	3/58
24813	11/49	28691	5/53	30628	4/58
24819	12/49	28734	6/53	30645	5/58
24835	1/50	28760	7/53	30681	6/58
24881	2/50	28786	8/53	30695	7/58
24919	3/50	28839	9/53	30705	8/58
24947	4/50	28875	10/53	30741	9/58
----------		28927	11/53	30749	10/58
25055	2/47	28961	12/53	30791	12/58
25076	6/47	29000	2/54	30819	1/59
25093	7/47	29069	3/54	30844	2/59
25230	9/47	29088	4/54	30850	3/59
25275	10/47	29123	5/54	30885	4/59
25289	11/47	29174	6/54	30897	5/59
25292	12/47	29194	7/54	30906	6/59
25336	1/48	29228	8/54	30939	7/59
25348	2/48	29249	9/54	30962	8/59
25357	4/48	29280	10/54	30965	9/59
25358	5/48	29326	11/54	30987	10/59
25395	7/48	29395	12/54	30999	11/59
25500	8/48	29403	2/55	31029	12/59
----------		29462	3/55	----------	
27024	5/50	29483	4/55	29131	3/44
27062	6/50	29520	5/55	29133	4/44
27084	7/50	29579	6/55	29142	10/44
27121	8/50	29593	7/55	29153	12/44
27185	9/50	29629	8/55	29173	7/45
27230	10/50	29653	9/55	29177	8/45
27245	11/50	29683	10/55	29178	1/46
27314	12/50	29733	11/55	29213	10/46

DECCA CON'T					
40000	11/45	46329	7/51	48195	2/51
40014	9/46	46341	8/51	48199	3/51
40039	7/47	46353	9/51	48210	4/51
40048	11/47	46368	10/51	48211	5/51
---------		46376	11/51	48218	6/51
45049	3/48	46382	12/51	48221	7/51
---------		46390	1/52	48227	8/51
		46396	2/52	48238	9/51
46022	1/47	46406	3/52	48243	10/51
46040	3/47	46407	4/52	48248	11/51
46041	4/47	---------		48256	12/51
46054	6/47	48012	9/46	48270	1/52
46061	7/47	48013	10/46	48274	2/52
46065	8/47	48016	1/47	48285	3/52
46073	10/47	48020	2/47	48287	10/52
46078	11/47	48025	4/47	48289	12/52
46090	12/47	48028	5/47	48290	4/53
46113	1/48	48029	7/47	48297	6/53
46115	2/48	48040	8/47	48298	7/53
46118	3/48	48047	9/47	48302	8/53
46119	4/48	48052	10/47	48303	10/53
46129	5/48	48057	11/47	48305	11/53
46133	6/48	48059	12/47	48308	1/54
46136	7/48	48069	1/48	48313	3/54
46140	9/48	48070	2/48	48315	4/54
46144	10/48	48073	3/48	48319	6/54
46145	11/48	48074	4/48	48320	7/54
46146	12/48	48078	5/48	48325	9/54
46148	2/49	48079	7/48	48326	10/54
46153	3/49	48086	9/48	48327	11/54
46157	4/49	48089	10/48	48329	12/54
46168	6/49	48090	11/48	48331	1/55
46170	7/49	48091	1/49	48332	3/55
46174	8/49	48093	2/49	48337	10/55
46180	9/49	48095	3/49		
46186	10/49	48100	4/49	(BRUNSWICK)	
46192	11/49	48103	5/49	55000	3/57
46196	12/49	48105	6/49	55004	4/57
46205	1/50	48108	7/49	55008	5/57
46218	2/50	48112	8/49	55009	6/57
46221	3/50	48115	9/49	55014	7/57
46225	4/50	48117	10/49	55020	8/57
46236	5/50	48119	11/49	55021	9/57
46246	6/50	48122	12/49	55030	10/57
46250	7/50	48124	1/50	55035	11/57
46254	8/50	48126	2/50	55044	12/57
46257	9/50	48138	3/50	55046	1/58
46268	10/50	48147	4/50	55054	2/58
46275	11/50	48156	5/50	55056	3/58
46280	12/50	48157	6/50	55059	4/58
46284	1/51	48163	7/50	55063	5/58
46289	2/51	48168	8/50	55072	6/58
46297	3/51	48169	9/50	55076	7/58
46300	4/51	48175	10/50	55083	8/58
46314	5/51	48181	11/50	55091	9/58
46326	6/51	48187	12/50	55095	10/58

DECCA CON'T		84030	5/54	60978	5/53
(BRUNSWICK)		84031	6/54	61009	6/53
55101	11/58	84032	10/54	61014	7/53
55107	12/58	----------		61028	8/53
55112	1/59	85002	1/48	61037	9/53
55114	2/59	SEE PAGE 157		61060	10/53
55120	3/59	(CORAL)		61093	11/53
55129	4/59	60000	11/48	61107	12/53
55130	5/59	60016	12/48	61125	1/54
55133	6/59	60024	3/49	61126	2/54
55137	7/59	60049	4/49	61136	3/54
55141	8/59	60066	6/49	61160	4/54
55147	9/59	60082	7/49	61171	5/54
55151	10/59	60091	8/49	61191	6/54
55156	11/59	60103	9/49	61201	7/54
----------		60120	10/49	61224	8/54
80000	1/43	60140	12/49	61240	9/54
80019	7/43	60147	1/50	61258	10/54
80043	11/43	60148	2/50	61301	11/54
80047	6/44	60161	3/50	61323	12/54
80055	7/44	60175	4/50	61339	1/55
80063	9/45	60213	5/50	61362	2/55
80073	12/45	60234	6/50	61379	3/55
80079	4/46	60239	7/50	61392	4/55
80089	6/47	60266	8/50	61423	5/55
80093	8/47	60294	9/50	61439	6/55
80103	3/49	60306	10/50	61467	7/55
80113	7/49	60334	11/50	61468	8/55
80114	9/49	60346	12/50	61498	9/55
80126	10/49	60354	1/51	61510	10/55
80133	2/50	60360	2/51	61530	11/55
80135	3/50	60404	3/51	61532	12/55
80138	4/50	60424	4/51	61567	1/56
80142	5/50	60446	5/51	61587	2/56
80147	6/50	60505	6/51	61609	3/56
80156	7/50	60521	7/51	61621	4/56
80158	11/50	60547	8/51	61644	5/56
80176	4/52	60565	9/51	61653	6/56
80222	7/53	60574	10/51	61670	7/56
80226	8/53	60592	11/51	61691	8/56
80229	9/53	60600	12/51	61702	9/56
80230	10/53	60626	1/52	61724	10/56
80233	11/53	60651	2/52	61748	11/56
80235	12/53	60659	3/52	61761	12/56
80236	2/54	60681	4/52	61779	1/57
80239	4/54	60737	6/52	61796	2/57
80241	5/54	60780	7/52	61811	3/57
80244	11/54	60804	8/52	61814	4/57
----------		60829	9/52	61837	5/57
84011	6/53	60849	10/52	61845	6/57
84015	8/53	60873	11/52	61856	7/57
84019	9/53	60894	12/52	61867	8/57
84022	10/53	60895	1/53	61879	9/57
84024	11/53	60921	2/53	61898	10/57
84025	3/54	60949	3/53	61908	11/57
84026	4/54	60963	4/53	61918	12/57

DECCA CON'T
  (CORAL)

61931	1/58	64118	2/52	65096	9/52	
61950	2/58	64122	3/52	65098	10/52	
61956	3/58	64123	5/52	65104	11/52	
61986	4/58	64132	6/52			
61991	5/58	64135	7/52	(DECCA-LONDON)		
61999	6/58	64136	8/52	41007	1/47	
62009	7/58	64138	9/52			
62025	8/58	64140	10/52	(VOCALION)		
62031	9/58	64143	11/52	55000	6/49	
62040	10/58	64147	3/53	55020	8/49	
62052	11/58	64152	4/53	55033	9/49	
62061	12/58	64154	5/53	55055	11/49	
62069	1/59	64160	8/53	55075	12/49	
62081	2/59	64162	9/53			
62094	3/59	64164	10/53			
62106	4/59	64171	2/54	DECOY		
62112	5/59	64173	4/54	1961	6/59	
62117	6/59	64174	6/54			
62130	7/59	64177	7/54	7105	12/58	
62134	8/59	64179	8/54			
62137	9/59	64180	9/54			
62146	10/59	64183	10/54	DECOY		
62156	11/59			7175	12/51	
62161	12/59	65000	11/48			
		65004	12/48			
64000	11/48	65005	3/49	DEED		
64004	12/48	65006	4/49	1002	4/55	
64005	3/49	65009	6/49	1004	7/55	
64008	4/49	65011	7/49	1006	9/55	
64010	6/49	65013	8/49	1011	2/56	
64013	7/49	65016	9/49	1015	3/56	
64016	8/49	65018	11/49	1016	4/56	
64021	9/49	65022	2/50	1019	5/56	
64022	10/49	65026	3/50			
64024	11/49	65029	4/50			
64029	2/50	65031	5/50	DEE DEE		
64035	4/50	65033	6/50	239	3/59	
64044	5/50	65035	7/50	241	7/59	
64046	6/50	65036	8/50			
64048	7/50	65037	9/50			
64053	8/50	65042	1/51	DEE GEE		
64060	9/50	65044	2/51	SEE SAVOY		
64061	10/50	65051	5/51			
64065	11/50	65054	6/51			
64069	12/50	65057	7/51	DEE JAY		
64072	1/51	65060	8/51	1247	3/57	
64076	2/51	65063	9/51			
64082	3/51	65064	10/51			
64087	4/51	65067	11/51	DELAWARE		
64094	6/51	65072	12/51	8636	12/58	
64099	7/51	65075	1/52			
64104	9/51	65077	2/52			
64111	10/51	65082	4/52	DELAWARE		
64115	1/52	65089	5/52		VALLEY	
		65091	6/52	100	7/59	
		65095	7/52			

DELCO
4002   9/59

DEL-FI
4101   1/58
4102   2/58
4103   3/58
4106   9/58
4109   11/58
4112   3/59
4116   5/59
4117   6/59
4119   7/59
4120   8/59
4125   10/59
4129   11/59
4132   12/59

(LARK)
455   3/58
456   5/58
459   10/58

4510   1/59

DELHI
101   4/53

DELL
5202   9/59

DELLA
117   8/53

DELMAC
1001   3/48

DEL PAT
206   4/59

DEL-RAY
136   1/59
----
201   2/58

DELTA
SEE BULLET

DELTA
D-10-1   9/44

DELTA
100   11/54

1002   2/59

1502   7/56

DEL-TONE
5012   5/58

DELUXE
SEE KING

DELVAR
107   9/49
111   10/49
114   12/49
117   3/50
----
502   1/50
503   3/50

DEM
101   1/54
----
408   3/55

1632   2/56

DEMO
1011   2/53
1039   10/59

DEMON
1503   3/58
1508   6/58
1509   8/58
1510   10/58
1511   11/58
1513   2/59
1516   4/59
1517   5/59
1519   8/59
1520   10/59
1521   12/59

1600   7/58

DENALU
2579   8/59

DENERE
317   5/58

DESIGN
818   5/58
820   9/58
827   12/58
829   1/59
830   2/59

DESTINY
402   12/58

DE WITT
10   8/57

7063   10/58

DERBY
712   6/49
713   7/49
717   9/49
723   11/49
725   12/49
728   2/50
737   4/50
741   7/50
747   9/50
748   10/50
754   2/51
760   4/51
761   6/51
766   8/51
772   9/51
777   11/51
786   12/51
787   1/52
790   3/52
791   4/52
793   5/52
796   6/52
800   7/52
807   9/52
809   10/52
813   11/52

DERBY CON'T
814	12/52
815	1/53
820	3/53
821	4/53
823	5/53
824	6/53
825	7/53
829	8/53
831	10/53
834	11/53
836	12/53
839	2/54
847	4/54
852	5/54
859	8/54

SEE PAGE 157

DEVON
1001	10/52

DIAL
100	4/59

125	1/59

DIAL
1001	4/46
1002	5/46
1005	11/46
1017	2/48
1031	1/49
1033	7/49

DIAMOND
1002	10/53

2054	1/47
2057	3/47
2078	4/47
2081	5/47
2084	10/47
2090	1/48

3001	4/56
3004	6/56
3008	9/56

DIANA
100	3/59

DICE
96	6/59

DIG
SEE ALADDIN

DIN
3439	9/59

DINAMO
1002	5/59
1004	7/59

DISC
SEE ASH

DISC-CO
100	6/50

DISC-CO
1001	12/58

DISC-JOCKEY
256	8/50

752	10/49

1002	10/49
1017	8/50

DISCOVERY
SEE SAVOY

DISNEYLAND
37	6/56
39	11/56
42	12/56
46	3/57
50	4/57
53	5/57
54	6/57
55	8/57
71	10/57
100	3/58
102	4/58
118	12/58
120	2/59

123	4/59
125	10/59

4012	3/56

(BUENA VISTA)
(VISTA)
331	9/58
332	11/58
333	2/59
336	3/59
337	5/59
341	7/59
345	8/59
346	9/59

DITTO
101	12/56
113	4/58
123	6/59

DIVA
1003	5/55

DIXIE
111	5/47

500	6/49

DIXIE
101	1/56

DIXIE
SEE STARDAY

DIXIE JUBILEE
104	4/58

DOE
SEE APOLLO

DOKE
102	5/59
103	12/58

502	5/59

DOLLIE
102   3/58
103   12/58

DOLLYANNA
101   10/55

DOLPHIN
SEE LIBERTY

DOLTON
SEE LIBERTY

DOME
252   6/49
----
810   8/49

1001   2/48
1004   10/48
1012   7/49
1014   8/49
1018   3/50
1019   7/50
1020   11/50
1030   12/51
1040   1/52
1050   7/52
1053   8/52
1054   9/52
1055   10/52
1058   2/53
1063   6/53
1066   12/53

DOME
501   5/58

DOMINANT
3000   11/57

DOMINO
308   12/49
----
350   5/50

DOMINO
500   7/58

600   10/58
----
800   10/58

1000   6/59

DOMINION
26   8/53

DOMME
022   11/57

DONICK
100   2/59

DONNA
3   5/57
----
104   10/59

1313   11/59

5733   7/56

DONNETT HIT
112   7/49
----
211   9/49
----
222   9/49
----
333   9/49
----
400   8/49
----
555   9/49
----
715   9/49
----
777   7/49

DOOTO
SEE BLUE

DOOTONE
SEE BLUE

DORAN
3515   8/59

D'ORO
101   12/52
103   2/53

DORE
SEE ERA

DO-RE-ME
1406   12/59

DORRINGTON
100   12/58

DOS
944   5/56

DOT
D-1   2/47
----
102   7/47

(DOWN HOME)
100   8/48
----
200   8/48
----
500   9/47

DOT
201   12/51

1001   1/50
1002   5/50
1003   6/50
1004   7/50
1010   9/50
1011   10/50
1014   11/50
1018   12/50
1028   2/51
1036   3/51
1053   5/51
1060   6/51
1069   9/51
1071   11/51
1073   12/51

DOT CON'T

1082	1/52
1091	3/52
1105	5/52
1116	8/52
1128	1/53
1129	2/53
1133	3/53
1135	4/53
1138	6/53
1141	7/53
1142	8/53
1143	10/53
1144	12/53
1189	3/54
1199	5/54
1210	8/54
1220	9/54
1224	10/54
1227	11/54
1231	12/54
1237	2/55
1243	4/55
1245	5/55
1262	7/55
1267	9/55
1271	11/55
1273	12/55
1275	2/56
1282	5/56
1283	6/56
1285	7/56
1286	10/56
1288	2/57
1289	4/57

15001	9/51
15002	10/51
15003	12/51
15004	1/52
15007	2/52
15010	3/52
15016	5/52
15020	7/52
15021	10/52
15034	11/52
15045	1/53
15055	2/53
15060	3/53
15062	4/53
15085	5/53
15091	6/53
15095	7/53
15102	8/53
15105	9/53
15107	10/53

15120	11/53
15127	1/54
15134	3/54
15163	5/54
15171	6/54
15220	7/54
15222	9/54
15247	10/54
15265	11/54
15318	1/55
15338	2/55
15347	3/55
15365	4/55
15370	5/55
15375	6/55
15386	7/55
15407	8/55
15412	9/55
15423	10/55
15435	11/55
15436	12/55
15443	1/56
15447	2/56
15451	3/56
15458	4/56
15463	5/56
15474	6/56
15481	7/56
15491	8/56
15499	9/56
15506	10/56
15511	11/56
15521	12/56
15537	1/57
15539	2/57
15545	3/57
15560	4/57
15579	5/57
15594	6/57
15601	7/57
15610	8/57
15636	9/57
15660	10/57
15666	11/57
15680	12/57
15688	1/58
15706	2/58
15708	3/58
15742	4/58
15755	5/58
15779	6/58
15791	7/58
15807	8/58
15825	9/58
15840	10/58
15855	11/58

15875	12/58
15894	1/59
15899	2/59
15914	3/59
15926	4/59
15950	5/59
15952	6/59
15964	7/59
15976	8/59
15983	9/59
15988	10/59
16002	11/59
16016	12/59

DOUBLE AA
SEE AA

DOUBLE FORTUNE
SEE TALENT

DOUBLE-PLAY

101	6/55

DOVE

236	3/58

DOVER

101	12/56

DOWN BEAT

128	4/48
159	10/48
168	2/49
171	3/49
189	4/49
205	5/49
(SWING BEAT)	
230	10/49
(SWING TIME)	
234	10/50
242	11/50
244	12/50
261	3/51
266	5/51
287	6/51
288	7/51
290	2/52
296	7/52
305	8/52

DOWN BEAT
(SWING TIME)
CON'T
306   9/52
311   10/52
317   11/52
322   1/53
327   2/53
330   4/53
345   2/54
(FLAME)
1004   5/53

DOWN BEAT
200   3/56
204   10/56

DOWN HOME
SEE DOT

DOWN HOME
7   10/50
12   12/50

DRAGON
106   4/58

DRAMA
102   9/54

DREAM
102   11/53

1001   8/59

1300   6/57

DREXEL
0601   10/54

DRUM
017   4/59

DRUMMOND
6000   5/54

DUB
2837   11/57
2838   12/57
2841   2/58
2842   3/58
2843   6/58

DUBONNET
4025   10/51

DUCKY
711   7/59

DUDE
0577   4/59

DUDLEY
500   4/50
----
601   12/49

1001   12/49

DUKE
110   5/45
114   8/45

DUKE
SEE PEACOCK

DWAIN
801   6/59
802   8/59
803   9/59

6072   4/59

DYNAMIC
201   11/49

DYNASTY
619   7/59
625   8/59
629   10/59

EAGLE
10-103   12/53
10-107   3/54
----
701   5/46
----
751   3/47
----
803   1/47
809   6/50

EAGLE
301   12/57

1006   4/58

2000   6/59

EARO
581   4/58

EARTH
1013   9/59

EASTMAN
779   3/56
787   10/58
790   2/59
791   4/59
792   5/59
793   6/59

EAST-WEST
SEE ATLANTIC

EASTY
102   5/50

EBB
100   5/57
105   6/57
107   7/57
109   8/57
115   10/57
120   11/57
123   12/57
130   2/58
142   3/58
145   4/58

EBB CON'T
146	6/58
147	7/58

EBONY
102	4/58
103	12/58

ECHO
106	7/50
111	9/50

ECHO
250	3/57

1001	8/55
1002	11/55
1003	2/56

ECHOIC
7031	10/56

17297	12/56

ECLIPSE
1651	4/57
1653	5/57
1655	11/57
1660	6/58

ECON
4501	8/59

EDISON INTERNATIONAL
401	8/58
409	4/59
410	8/59
411	9/59
412	10/59
414	11/59

EDSEL
778	5/59

E K
100	10/59

EKKO
101	7/54
108	10/54
112	1/55
115	6/55
116	8/55

1000	3/55
1004	6/55
1015	10/55
1020	11/55
1023	2/56

3001	6/56

20001	10/55

EKO
501	4/58
503	6/58
505	8/58
506	11/58

ELDORADO
SEE LUNIVERSE

ELECTRA
ELEKTRA
1	3/57
2	4/57
7	11/59

ELGIN
005	2/59
020	5/59

ELITE
SEE VARSITY

ELMAR
101	8/55

ELMONT
1001	8/58

ELSAN
1002	7/58
1003	9/58

1004	11/58
1006	5/59

ELVITRUE
2141	9/57

11575	7/57

EMARCY
SEE MERCURY

EMBASSY
104	12/48

5-1001	1/48
1005	2/48
1006	6/48
1009	8/48

11031	5/48

15004	2/48

EMBASSY
2400	4/55

EMBEE
1001	7/57

EMBER
SEE HERALD

EMBLEM
209	9/56

EMC
901	5/59

968	12/59

EMERALD
101	8/46
106	1/47

EMERALD
1998	7/54

EMERALD CON'T
2002   10/54
2004   3/55
2007   10/55
2010   5/56
2011   7/56

7071   1/52

8111   7/52
8118   8/52

9444   6/53

9966   5/54

EMGE
1005   8/58

EMPEROR
55   6/55
----
112   3/57
113   5/58
----
202   11/55
----
300   2/59
----
459   6/59

EMPEY
101   1/47
102   2/47
105   1/50
----
881   12/49

EMPIRE
101   3/56
103   6/56
107   10/56
----
759   4/59

EMPIRE
502   8/50
----
692   7/45

1000   8/50

EMPIRICAL
5   10/54

ENCINO
1007   4/57
1018   6/57

ENCORE
500   3/46

END
SEE ROULETTE

ENRICA
121   10/59

1002   8/59

ENSIGN
SEE KEEN

ENTERPRISE
107   3/57

1182   7/57
1208   1/58
1211   6/58
1226   4/59
1232   6/59
1234   7/59

ENTERPRISE
175   8/46
----
243   1/47
273   6/47
285   7/47
295   8/47
----
416   12/49

1101   7/47

1502   7/47

ENTRE
102   4/53

EPIC
SEE COLUMBIA

EQUITY
1003   3/54

ERA
1000   4/55
1001   6/55
1003   7/55
1004   10/55
1007   11/55
1008   12/55
1009   1/56
1010   2/56
1011   3/56
1013   4/56
1016   5/56
1017   7/56
1019   8/56
1020   10/56
1023   11/56
1026   12/56
1028   2/57
1031   3/57
1033   4/57
1036   4/57
1039   7/57
1041   8/57
1044   9/57
1045   10/57
1048   11/57
1056   1/58
1060   2/58
1064   3/58
1067   5/58
1075   7/58
1079   8/58
1080   9/58
1087   11/58
1088   1/59
1092   4/59

3000   6/59
3002   7/59
3003   8/59
3005   9/59

20001   7/56

(DORE)
500   6/58
501   7/58
503   9/58

ERA (DORE)		288	9/57	106	4/55
CON'T		297	8/59	109	7/55
516	2/59	---------		111	10/55
517	3/59	784	3/58	112	3/56
520	5/59	---------		123	5/57
522	6/59	1001	8/59	124	6/57
524	7/59	---------		125	7/57
531	10/59	9592	10/58		

		ETNA		**EXCELLENT**	
ERALD	9/59	1309	10/50	202	8/52
2052		---------		203	1/53
		1505	10/49	213	2/55
EIRE				221	9/55
191	12/58			226	12/55
		EVANS		---------	
		610	8/57	310	8/56
ERWIN				---------	
555	12/57			415	2/55
---------		**EVENT**		---------	
3777	10/57	4256	5/56	503	7/56
		4257	9/56		
		4258	11/56		
ESA		4260	2/57	**EXCELLO**	
1027	1/57	4261	5/57	1005	9/51
		4263	6/57	1007	12/51
		4267	9/57	---------	
ESCO		4274	4/58	2000	8/52
100	4/59	4275	6/58	2010	5/53
104	9/59	4287	10/58	2016	7/53
		4288	11/58	2017	10/53
		4289	12/58	2020	11/53
ESQUIRE		4292	3/59	2022	12/53
100	1/47	4294	5/59	2024	1/54
---------				2026	3/54
1113	4/50			2031	4/54
1127	12/53			2035	6/54
1129	3/54	**EVEREST**		2038	7/54
1133	2/55	19301	6/59	2042	9/54
1136	12/55	19315	9/59	2047	11/54
1137	6/56	19316	10/59	2048	1/55
1148	7/56	19319	11/59	2053	2/55
		19321	12/59	2055	3/55
				2057	4/55
ESSEX				2058	5/55
SEE PALDA		**EVERLAST**		2059	7/55
		5001	6/57	2062	9/55
				2066	10/55
ESTA				2069	11/55
100	8/59	**EVERSTATE**		2070	12/55
---------		101	11/49	2073	1/56
279	8/56	121	1/50	2074	2/56
281	11/56			2076	3/56
282	12/56	**EXCEL**		2077	4/56
284	6/57	104	2/55	2080	6/56
				2084	7/56

EXCELLO CON'T		EXCELSIOR			
2089	8/56	545	4/54	2986	11/44
2090	9/56	546	7/54	----------	
2092	11/56	547	11/54	(EXCLUSIVE)	
2097	12/56	548	1/55	10x	12/46
2099	1/57	550	2/55	13x	5/47
2105	2/57	551	4/55	16x	6/47
2106	4/57	555	5/55	17x	8/47
2108	5/57	557	7/55	19x	9/47
2111	7/57	562	9/55	25x	11/47
2118	8/57	564	10/55	26x	1/48
2120	9/57	565	11/55	29x	3/48
2123	11/57	568	12/55	31x	5/48
2129	2/58	569	2/56	37x	6/48
2136	4/58	574	3/56	45x	8/48
2140	6/58	575	4/56	51x	10/48
2141	8/58	579	6/56	61x	11/48
2144	10/58	582	7/56	68x	12/48
2145	11/58	585	9/56	77x	1/49
2146	12/58	589	11/56	79x	2/49
2150	2/59	593	1/57	83x	3/49
2154	4/59	594	2/57	93x	5/49
2156	5/59	596	3/57	103x	6/49
2158	6/59	599	5/57	107x	7/49
2160	7/59	601	6/57	----------	
2161	8/59	604	7/57	201	3/45
2164	9/59	607	9/57	208	7/45
2168	10/59	610	10/57	209	11/45
----------		614	3/58	217	4/46
(NASCO)		617	5/58	218	5/46
1002	4/59	620	6/58	219	6/46
----------		623	8/58	223	7/46
6000	5/57	625	9/58	227	8/46
6003	7/57	628	11/58	232	10/46
6005	4/57	631	12/58	234	11/46
6008	4/58	637	3/59	235	12/46
6012	5/58	640	6/59	236	1/47
6014	7/58	644	7/59	238	2/47
6019	9/58	648	10/59	239	4/47
6021	10/58	654	11/59	246	6/47
6022	11/58			249	8/47
6023	12/58			250	9/47
6024	2/59	EXCELSIOR		252	11/47
6026	4/59	101	7/44	255	12/47
6027	5/59	103	10/44	258	1/48
6028	6/59	105	3/45	261	2/48
6029	8/59	111	4/45	263	3/48
6030	12/59	130	9/45	268	5/48
----------		141	11/45	271	6/48
(NASHBORO)		149	1/46	----------	
512	9/51	150	3/46	700	12/46
516	12/51	174	5/46	703	4/47
522	10/52	175	8/46	----------	
535	5/53	----------		3113	2/44
540	7/53	500	2/47	----------	
544	12/53	532	1/49	(CLASS)	
		536	5/49	101	12/51

EXCELSIOR
(CLASS) CON'T

201	9/56
202	10/56
205	11/56
208	5/57
209	6/57
211	8/57
213	9/57
214	11/57
215	12/57
217	1/58
219	2/58
224	3/58
226	4/58
227	5/58
229	6/58
233	7/58
234	8/58
238	10/58
241	11/58
243	2/59
246	3/59
249	4/59
254	6/59
257	9/59
259	10/59
260	11/59
263	12/59

501	3/53

1060	6/58

2111	7/59

EXCELSIOR

1314	6/51
1315	7/51

EXCLUSIVE
SEE EXCELSIOR

01	2/59

10-02	5/59

100	6/58

501	9/57

EXITO

20-322	1/52

1507	2/50

EXPRESS

501	2/59

E-Z

684	7/55
685	11/55

FABLE

501	9/55
546	11/56
583	5/57
587	7/57
590	8/57
599	11/57
609	2/58
637	8/58
665	7/59

FABOR
SEE ABBOTT

FABULOUS

286	7/58

FACINATION

2000	12/58

FAIRFIELD

101	9/59

FAITH

1000	1/59

FALCON
SEE VEE JAY

FAME

101	2/59

313	5/59

501	12/57
503	5/58
504	5/59
506	11/59

FAMOUS

600	11/47
602	1/48
606	3/48

901	1/48

FAN
SEE JET

FANART

21308	7/56

F & L

101	8/53

F & P

1001	5/50

FANFARE

102	5/49
104	8/49
107	9/49

180	1/50

502	8/49
506	8/50

FANFARE

711	8/58

FANG

1001	6/59

FANTASY

503	6/50
511	11/50
513	2/51
514	5/51
518	3/52
519	6/52
526	7/53
528	12/53
530	3/54
536	8/55
539	9/55
543	4/59

FANTASY CON'T
719   9/55
720   10/55

F.A.R.
11   2/57

FARGO
1001   3/58
1002   6/58
1003   9/58
1004   11/58
1005   2/59
1006   3/59

FARGO
1110   9/45

FARO
584   11/58
585   1 /58
587   1/59
592   3/59
594   7/59
596   8/59

FAVORITE
1000   8/43

FAVORITE
21000   11/54

FAYETTE
1001   4/55

FDS PARADISE
1   8/55

FEATURE
1001   4/44
1003   7/44
1005   10/44
1007   12/44
1008   1/45
1009   2/45

FEATURE
2002   1/49
2012   3/49

FEATURE
1077   1/54
1089   3/54

FEDERAL
SEE KING

FEE BEE
223   5/58

FELCO
101   2/59
102   5/59
104   8/59
----
201   8/59
----
301   8/59

FELSTED
8500   11/57
8502   12/57
8504   1/58
8508   2/58
8513   3/58
8514   4/58
8518   5/58
8523   6/58
8537   8/58
8543   9/58
8544   10/58
8545   11/58
8549   1/59
8556   2/59
8570   3/59
8572   5/59
8582   6/59
8587   7/59
8591   8/59
8594   10/59
8596   11/59

FERN
746   12/58
776   6/59

FERNWOOD
1   5/59
----
107   6/58
108   8/58
109   10/58
111   4/59
113   6/59
114   9/59
115   11/59

FIDELITY
711   7/47

2000   7/47

3000   7/47

FIDELITY
SEE SPECIALTY
PAGE   157

FIESTA
10-011   6/53

20-028   2/54
----
47   4/55
52   6/55
062   2/56
063   3/56
064   4/56
066   5/56
074   12/56
097   11/58
100   5/59
101   6/59

FILMTOWN
           HOLLYWOOD
102   4/54

FINCH
2001   8/59

FINE
1001   7/49
1005   5/50
1009   2/51
1011   2/52

FINE
55-3-31 5/55

1001   6/55
1003   11/55
1010   6/56

1857   7/57

FINE ART
207   11/58

FINE ART
1001   12/48
1002   5/49
1003   7/49

FINESS
1717   12/59

FINK'S
RECORDS
2732   12/58

FIRE
SEE FURY

FIRESIDE
101   3/50

FIRESIDE
28836   5/57
28837   1/58
28838   5/58

FIRST
103   2/59
104   6/59

F.J.T.
1073   1/53

FLAGSHIP
57A   10/57
----
105   4/58

914   10/57

FLAIR
SEE MODERN

FLAIR-X
3000   10/56
3002   12/56
3008   1/57

5000   1/57
5003   2/57
5004   3/57

FLAME
SEE DOWN BEAT

FLAME
101   9/58
110   12/58
111   4/58
----
154   4/58
----
305   9/59

1018   8/59

FLAMINGO
3993   7/56

FLASH
SEE PALDA

FLASH
108   5/56
110   9/56
112   10/56
114   11/56
116   5/57
123   8/57
127   2/58
128   3/58
130   10/58
133   3/59

FLEETWOOD
1001   6/58

FLINT
1782   8/48
1789   9/48

5005   4/48
5011   5/48

15002   1/48

FLIP
SEE SUN

FLIP
302   4/55
320   1/57
321   4/57
322   5/57
325   9/57
327   12/57
331   3/58
333   4/58
334   5/58
335   7/58
336   8/58
338   9/58
339   10/58
340   12/58
343   3/59
344   4/59
345   4/59
346   6/59
347   7/59
348   12/59

1001   4/57

FLIPPIN'
201   7/59
202   11/59

FLORENCE
1001   8/53

FLORIDA
X99   12/48
----
999   1/48

FLOTO
78003   4/53

FLYING SAUCER
501   10/57

FM
261   1/48
264   10/48

FOCUS
1011   4/56

FOLK STAR
103   8/50
----
500   11/49
----
601   10/50
609   7/51

FOLKWAYS
SEE ASH

FOLLY
800   12/58

FORD
100   11/58
101   2/59

FORECAST
102   4/54
115   8/54
----
301   5/55

5002   6/54

FOREMOST
101   3/57
115   11/57

1003   11/56

FOREST
1005   8/54

FOREST
5601   6/56
5602   7/56
5603   8/56

FOREST CITY
1000   11/53
1001   5/54
1003   6/54

FOREVER
1803   12/58

FORMAL
1001   2/56

FORTE
314   7/59

FORTUNE
101   9/46
106   10/48
112   6/49
116   8/49
117   9/49
122   10/49
123   11/49
130   12/49
141   3/50
142   8/50
145   11/50
155   3/51
161   9/51
166   6/52
170   1/53
173   7/53
175   11/53
176   2/54
178   9/54
181   11/54
184   9/55
185   2/56
187   9/56
----
508   2/54
509   4/54
511   9/54
514   3/55
516   5/55
518   10/55
519   5/56

522   11/56
525   5/57
531   2/59
----
711   3/51
----
800   5/50
805   9/51
806   12/51
807   5/52
809   5/53
820   9/55
824   10/55
825   2/56
828   9/56
833   4/57
837   8/57
839   12/57

"45"
5413   5/59

FORWARD
313   5/59

FOTO
SEE MILTONE

FOUR STAR
101   8/45

1002   8/45
1008   10/45
1026   11/45
1038   2/46
1055   3/46
1079   4/46
1083   5/46
1117   6/46
1131   7/46
1136   8/46
1138   9/46
1144   11/46
1151   1/47
1169   9/47
1225   1/48
1230   6/48
1254   7/48
1259   8/48
1271   9/48
1274   10/48
1282   12/48

FOUR STAR
CON'T

1289	2/49
1292	4/49
1312	6/49
1339	10/49
1376	11/49
1386	12/49
1397	1/50
1414	2/50
1442	3/50
1458	4/50
1460	5/50
1475	6/50
1504	7/50
1510	8/50
1516	9/50
1529	10/50
1540	11/50
1550	2/51
1553	3/51
1564	6/51
1570	8/51
1574	9/51
1580	11/51
1591	2/52
1601	4/52
1608	5/52
1613	8/52
1617	10/52
1624	1/53
1630	3/53
1638	6/53
1641	8/53
1645	11/53
1649	1/54
1651	2/54
1653	3/54
1655	5/54
1661	6/54
1664	9/54
1678	7/55
1681	11/55
1699	11/56
1700	4/57
1708	7/57
1710	8/57
1711	9/57
1714	1/58
1721	5/58
1729	1/59
1730	5/59
1732	9/59
1733	10/59

X-84	3/54

86	5/54
X-93	6/54
96	9/54
100	10/55
(BIG TOWN)	
103	5/53
106	7/53
107	10/53
110	10/53
111	2/54

408	10/54

1005	5/53

(GILT EDGE)	
X-15	6/51

GE 18	5/54
GE 21	9/54
GE 22	11/54
T 23	11/55

221	4/45

500GG-1	10/44
(501)	
500CG-11	12/44
(503)	
504	3/45
505	6/45
508	9/45
517	10/45
532	2/46
536	3/46
539	4/46

5004	3/50
5015	10/50
5026	2/51
5029	3/51
5039	6/51
5049	11/51
5052	12/51
5058	2/52
5064	4/52
5066	5/52
5068	8/52
5071	9/52
5075	10/52
5077	12/52
5082	3/53
5092	4/55
5094	7/55
5095	11/55

FOUR WINDS
2003	9/58

FOX
1	12/57
3	2/58
5	4/58
6	7/58

405	6/55
407	7/55
408	12/55
409	5/57

FRAN-TONE
2004	12/45

FRANKIE
4	3/58
5	5/58

FRANTIC
111	4/59
112	6/59

751	2/59

FRANTIE
110	1/59

FRANWILL
100	12/46

600	9/47

701	11/50

5011	5/50
5012	7/50
5016	5/54
5027	1/56

FRANZ SCHUBERT
432	10/54
444	3/57
445	2/58
446	4/58
447	12/58

FRATERNITY
715   7/55
731   2/56
734   3/56
738   5/56
739   6/56
741   7/56
750   10/56
751   11/56
755   3/57
758   3/57
777   7/57
778   9/57
784   11/57
796   2/58
799   3/58
802   4/58
805   5/58
817   7/58
824   10/58
837   3/59
842   4/59
844   5/59
852   7/59
857   9/59
860   10/59

1008   11/58

(CO-ED)
049   6/56
094   8/59
----
110   11/45
115   12/51
126   6/55
132   10/56
----
214   6/47
----
409   5/49
----
503   7/58
504   10/58
506   11/58
508   1/59
512   5/59
515   7/59
518   10/59
522   12/59

1960   12/59

(SORORITY)
105   11/43

FRIENDLY
100   4/58
105   5/58

1010   12/57

1100   9/58

FROLIC
100   8/49

FRONTIER
101   8/49
103   12/50

FRONTIER
297   6/59

FULTON
1254   5/54

FUNNY FACE
100   1/47

FURY
1003   9/57
1010   3/58
1023   3/59

(FIRE)
100   4/56
105   6/56
111   7/56
116   8/56

1000   8/59
1008   12/59

(ROBIN)
105   1/52
5001   12/51

(RED ROBIN)
114   5/53
115   6/53
125   2/54

(WHIRLIN DISC)
100   8/56

102   12/56
105   3/57
107   7/57

FUTURA
3003   7/49

FUTURA
10001 6/59

FUTURAMA
3009   1/50

FUTURE
2200   1/58
2201   3/58
2203   7/58

GAARE
103   11/52

GAIN
103   3/59

GAITY
161   7/59
169   8/59

GALA
20   1/47
----
194   12/45
200   1/48

1000   8/43
1022   1/48

2604   1/48

3550   6/47

5001   2/48

GALA
101   3/59
104   6/59
105   8/59

GALA CON'T
106   9/59

GALAXY
701   9/51
704   6/52
705   11/52

GALE
101   3/57
102   4/57

GALLANT
2001   5/59

GALLO
103   12/57
105   3/58
108   7/58

GAME TIME
103   9/57
108   4/59

G & F
102   7/58
104   9/58

G & G
122   3/59
126   4/59

GAP
795   12/49

GARNETT
500   3/54

GATEWAY
3006   9/53

GAYLO
100   5/58
102   5/59

GEE
SEE TICO

GEM
1   8/45
9   9/45
15   11/45
----
510   6/49
----
615   11/45
----
713   6/48

1500   1/48

(JEWEL)
1000   10/45
1004   8/46

1200   8/48

2002   5/48
2007   8/48

3000   10/45
3004   6/49

4000   10/48

5000   10/45

7003   6/49

GEM
SEE SAVOY

GEM-TONE
100   8/59
----
750   10/58
751   8/59

GENE NORMAN
           PRESENTS
115   11/56

GENERAL
1706   2/40

GENIE
104   1/59

1301   4/55
1302   5/57

GENNETT
SEE BEACON

GEORGIAN
1630   12/59

GG
1017   4/46
1028   5/46
1029   6/46

G G
101   9/55
----
518   12/55

GI
101   4/46

G. I.
1252   9/56

GIANT
1808   2/59

5001   3/57
5005   5/57

GIBRALTER
101   5/55
102   3/59

GIG
200   5/56
----
300   9/57

GIGI
1   3/59

GILT EDGE
SEE FOUR STAR

GINCHEE
101   9/59

1002   9/59

GIRA
025   11/58
030   8/59

GIZMO
102   2/55
----
561   8/56
581   7/58

GLAD
109   10/58

GLEN
102   7/58

GLENN
1401   9/59

1501   9/59

1800   9/59

GLO
5193   8/59

GLOBAL
715   3/58
716   5/58
717   8/58
720   3/59
721   8/59

GLOBE
102   8/45
104   11/45
107   1/46
110   4/46

GLOBE
1258   4/59

GLORY
SEE KING

GLORY
234   6/55
236   10/55
238   1/56
241   4/56
242   6/56
244   8/56
247   9/56
248   10/56
249   12/56
250   1/57
252   2/57
256   3/57
257   4/57
259   5/57
260   6/57
264   9/57
266   11/57
268   12/57
270   1/58
272   2/58
274   3/58
276   5/58
283   9/58
290   12/58
293   5/59
298   7/59
299   11/59

GLOVER
200   10/59

GLOW-HILL
500   10/57
503   7/58
505   8/59

GMP
929   2/55

GNP
122   5/57
127   9/57
130   2/58

131   4/58
133   6/58
136   9/58
140   3/59
142   5/59

GO
103   6/58

GOLD
733   10/58
734   6/59

GOLDBAND
1019   11/50
1030   3/56
1070   8/58
1078   12/58
1086   4/59
1088   6/59
1091   8/59

GOLDEN
42   2/50

GOLDEN
550   8/59

GOLDEN CREST
10   7/57
----
104   5/57
107   6/57
114   9/57
124   1/58
----
302   12/59
----
501   5/58
502   6/58
505   8/58
507   9/58
512   1/59
515   3/59
526   7/59

1231   11/57
1282   2/58
1301   3/58
1321   4/58

GOLDEN ROD
14	1/52
45	12/56

103	6/54

202	10/56

300	6/57

500	8/57
501	11/57

GOLD METAL
929	9/48
942	12/48
946	1/49
954	9/49

GOLD RAIN
107	12/49
121	11/51

GOLD SEAL
333	12/47

660	12/47

2001	3/47

2327	4/48

3003	1/48

3501	1/48

GOLD STAR
105	2/54

GOLD STAR
135	4/49

501	8/49
502	11/49

652	3/49
656	6/49
661	8/49
665	11/49

715	11/49

1318	3/47
1380	11/49

GOLD-TONE
1001	3/48
1022	6/50

GO-LISH
101	12/55

GONE
SEE ROULETTE

GONG
1	2/49

GOOD TIME
JAZZ	
33	5/51
50	2/52
64	7/52
71	10/52
78	4/53
82	7/53
85	9/53
87	11/53
89	12/53

4509	3/55

GOODE
3963	4/58
3966	8/58

GOODY
SEE GOTHAM

GOSPEL
SEE PALDA

GOSPEL
SEE SAVOY

GOSPEL
JUBILEE	
501	10/56

503	11/56
505	10/57
511	4/59
513	5/59

GOTHAM
100	4/46
107	5/46
108	7/46
122	8/46
151	8/47
154	1/48
160	3/48
161	6/48
162	9/48
163	10/48
166	11/48
170	1/49
172	3/49
175	4/49
178	5/49
181	7/49
188	8/49
192	9/49
194	10/49
201	11/49
205	12/49
227	4/50
231	5/50
235	6/50
248	9/50
255	12/50
272	8/51
276	12/51
279	3/52
282	5/52
284	9/52
290	3/53
294	5/53
318	6/56

410	8/51
412	10/51
413	11/51
423	4/52
428	7/52
435	2/53

500	4/46
501	5/46
506	12/50

602	1/49
603	3/49
606	5/49

GOTHAM CON'T
610	7/49
619	9/49
620	11/49
625	12/49
638	5/50
640	6/50
715	7/52
723	1/53
729	2/53
734	3/53
738	5/53
741	8/53

805	10/50

900	4/46

(APEX)
1105	4/49
1118	10/49
1119	11/49

(PHENIX)
1100	1/49
1102	2/49

(GOODY)
3000	2/46

(MUSIC MASTER)
20-97	9/49

(20TH CENTURY)
20-23	1/47
20-32	2/47
20-40	6/47
20-56	1/48
20-58	3/48
20-60	6/48
20-73	11/48
20-74	12/48
20-78	1/49
20-80	2/49
20-81	3/49
20-94	5/49
20-96	9/49
20-98	10/49
20-99	11/49
2100	3/50

1001	3/46

5000	3/52
5035	7/55

GOURE
5074	9/59

GRAMERCY
1061	5/52

GRAND
101	12/53
112	8/54
114	10/54
120	1/55
124	4/55
126	7/55
131	9/55
135	2/56
139	5/56

502	10/54

GRAND
2000	8/57
2001	1/59
2002	3/59

GRAND
973	11/48

25004	4/48
25011	12/48
25013	3/49
25014	4/49
25015	2/50

GRAND AWARD
1	3/56

1001	4/56
1003	5/56
1006	6/56
1008	2/57
1015	8/57
1018	9/57
1020	10/58
1025	1/59
1028	4/59
1032	5/59
1035	10/59

GREAT
103	9/59

487	12/58

GREAT LAKES
1201	1/54
1203	2/54

GREENBRIAR
115	5/57

11313	4/55

GREEN LABEL
22510	3/55

GREENWICH
41	12/58

408	4/58

GREGORIAN
101	2/57

GREGORIAN
2203	5/51
2207	9/53

GRENOBLE
805	3/53

1801	4/53

GREY CLIFF
721	6/59

GROOVE
SEE RCA VIC.

GUARANTEED
SEE CARLTON

GUIDE
1002	11/58

GUILD

101	3/45
114	5/45
122	9/45
140	10/45
148	11/45

1001	3/45
1003	10/45

GUILD

1831	11/52
1833	10/54
1900	9/58

GUITAR

101	3/59

GULF

100	9/45

GUYDEN

002	7/55

100	12/54
101	3/55

200	6/55

702	1/54
703	5/54
706	10/54
710	11/54
714	3/55

1043	7/57

2001	8/58
2004	9/58
2006	12/58
2010	2/59
2012	3/59
2014	4/59
2017	7/59
2022	8/59
2028	9/59

(JAMIE)	
1042	6/57

1101	3/58
1104	5/58

1107	7/58
1109	8/58
1110	10/58
1113	12/58
1116	1/59
1118	2/59
1120	3/59
1125	5/59
1128	6/59
1131	7/59
1135	10/59
1139	11/59
1148	12/59

HALLMARK

2000	3/58

HAMILTON

100	11/52
149	8/53

1025	5/53

HAMILTON

5005	10/58
5006	11/58

50001	12/58
50027	2/59
50030	3/59

HAMMOND

104	9/59

HAMP-TONE

100	6/46
104	7/46

HANOVER
SEE SIGNITURE

HANSEN

101	6/55
102	10/55
105	11/55

333	10/59

HAPPINESS

101	9/49
103	10/49
104	2/50
106	3/50

HARDMAN

4011	6/49
4015	7/49
4018	9/49

HARLEM
SEE SOUTHERN

HARLEM
SEE CASTLE

HARLEQUIN

401	3/57

HARMAD

103	4/55
104	6/55
108	3/56
110	5/56
112	6/56

HARMAND

101	6/54
102	8/54
106	10/55

HARMONIA

165	11/48

1098	8/45

1507	12/44

1701	8/48
1702	10/48

1908	10/47
1917	12/47
1921	7/48

5005	10/47

HARMONICA
811   2/48

HARMONY
SEE COLUMBIA

HARMONY
204   8/56

HARMONY
3001   5/52
3002   6/52

HARPER
4501   10/56

HARRINGTON
103   7/59

HARRISON
100   8/58

HART
1001   2/59

HARTBYRNE
1164   5/59

HART-VAN
2-0017   5/50
2-0114   4/52

2150   3/50

16003   5/49
16005   11/49
16011   12/49
16017   7/50
16022   11/50
16023   2/51

17002   3/50

HARVARD
1003   12/48

HARVARD
804   6/59
811   11/59

HARVEST
1501   1/59

HAVEN
108   1/56

HAVEN
500   6/46
508   10/46
----
800   6/46
803   10/46

1000   6/46
1001   10/46

3000   10/46

HAV-RAY
1151   4/52

HAWK
108   8/52

HEADLINE
101   8/55

1001   4/58
1004   8/59
1008   12/59

HEADLINE
116   3/48

HEART
1000   6/55

5001   9/59

HEART
1015   11/48

HEART BEAT
711   12/59

HEG
501   6/56

HEP
2002   6/58

2140   9/58

HERALD
408   5/53
414   6/53
415   7/53
416   8/53
417   9/53
419   11/53
420   1/54
421   2/54
424   3/54
425   4/54
427   5/54
430   6/54
432   7/54
433   8/54
435   9/54
439   11/54
443   12/54
444   1/55
445   2/55
449   3/55
452   4/55
454   5/55
455   6/55
458   7/55
461   9/55
463   10/55
466   12/55
470   1/56
471   2/56
472   3/56
474   4/56
476   5/56
480   6/56
481   7/56
485   8/56
488   10/56
491   11/56
492   12/56
494   2/57
497   3/57
498   4/57

HERALD CON'T	
503	5/57
504	6/57
505	8/57
506	9/57
507	10/57
508	11/57
510	12/57
513	1/58
517	3/58
518	4/58
519	5/58
521	6/58
524	7/58
525	8/58
528	9/58
531	11/58
534	12/58
536	2/59
542	9/59

| 1000 | 7/54 |

| 2003 | 1/55 |

(EMBER)

| 101 | 3/56 |

1003	5/56
1005	6/56
1006	8/56
1007	9/56
1008	10/56
1010	11/56
1011	12/56
1012	2/57
1015	4/57
1017	5/57
1019	6/57
1021	8/57
1025	10/57
1027	11/57
1029	12/57
1031	3/58
1034	5/58
1038	7/58
1039	8/58
1041	9/58
1044	10/58
1045	11/58
1047	12/58
1049	1/59
1052	5/59
1056	10/59

HERB JEFFIES PRESENTS

| 101 | 4/56 |

HI

| 423 | 5/56 |

HI

2001	12/57
2002	4/58
2006	8/58
2010	12/58
2014	3/59
2016	5/59
2018	10/59

HICKORY

1001	2/54
1004	3/54
1008	5/54
1012	8/54
1014	9/54
1017	11/54
1019	1/55
1023	5/55
1027	7/55
1029	8/55
1032	9/55
1034	10/55
1036	11/55
1038	12/55
1040	1/56
1044	3/56
1047	4/56
1050	5/56
1051	7/56
1052	8/56
1053	9/56
1055	10/56
1057	11/56
1058	1/57
1061	2/57
1064	5/57
1065	6/57
1066	7/57
1067	9/57
1069	10/57
1070	11/57
1073	12/57
1074	2/58
1075	3/58
1076	4/58
1080	6/58

1083	8/58
1085	10/58
1090	12/58
1095	3/59
1097	4/59
1100	6/59
1101	7/59
1102	8/59
1105	9/59
1107	10/59
1110	11/59

HI-Class

| 105 | 1/59 |

HIDUS

| 2008 | 5/55 |

HIDE-A-WAY

| 103 | 9/58 |

HI-FI

502	3/56
503	5/56
550	5/59
568	8/59
574	10/59

HI-FIRE

| 1001 | 8/58 |

HIGH TIME

98	7/49
118	9/49
132	4/50
145	8/50
150	12/50
176	5/56
177	5/57

HIGH WAY

| 1007 | 12/56 |

HIGHWAY

3456	6/48
3457	11/48
3459	1/49

HILITE
102   7/54
104   10/54
107   11/54
110   8/55

HILIWAY
70   6/53

HILL & COUNTRY
SEE APOLLO

HILLAIT
12054   4/51

HILLBILLY
71101   8/50
71104   9/50
71107   1/53
71111   6/53
71112   8/53

HILLCREST
200   6/59
- - - - - - - - -
778   8/58

HI-LO
1402   4/52
1407   5/52
1411   6/52
1412   9/52
1414   11/52
1417   3/53
1420   6/53

HILTON
0007   11/58
- - - - - - - - -
1002   8/57

HIP
302   11/56
- - - - - - - - -
501   8/57

HIT
SEE VARSITY

HIT
101   8/54

HIT
3000   12/58

HIT OF THE
MONTH CLUB
1298   3/48

HI-TONE
SEE SIGNITURE

HIT PARADE
501   8/52

HITS
504   1/47

HITT
179   10/58
180   11/58
182   12/58
183   7/59
184   8/59

HIT-TONE
240   11/49

H L
1   10/49

H. N. SOCIETY
101   8/45

HOB NOB
1954   4/54

HOBO
745   12/58

HOFFMAN C.L.W.
21372   3/54
21373   11/54

HOLIDAY
SEE PALDA

HOLIDAY
69   5/53

HOLIDAY
101   6/48
- - - - - - - - -
1001   10/49
- - - - - - - - -
2001   11/48
- - - - - - - - -
3001   10/48

HOLIDAY
2005   5/57
- - - - - - - - -
2605   6/57
2607   9/57

HOLLIS
1001   9/57

HOLLYWOOD
180   4/52
221   6/52
234   8/52
244   2/53
- - - - - - - - -
401   2/53
404   3/53
- - - - - - - - -
1001   11/53
1004   12/53
1006   1/54
1009   2/54
1010   3/54
1011   4/54
1014   5/54
1016   7/54
1018   10/54
1030   2/55
1034   5/55
1045   12/55
1051   2/56

HOLLYWOOD
CON'T
1055   3/56
1057   5/56
1065   9/56
1070   12/56
1077   4/57
1080   5/57
1081   6/57
1086   3/58
1089   4/58
1094   11/58
1097   5/59
1098   6/59
1099   7/59
1100   10/59

(HOLLYWOOD
          STAR)
798   12/54

(RECORDED IN
     HOLLYWOOD)
143   2/51
149   3/51
166   10/51
172   12/51

HOLLYWOOD
     RHYTHMS
1525   5/47
1532   7/47

1653   4/48

(SKATING
     RHYTHMS)
199   1/47

HOLMES
201   5/59

HOLMES RHYTHM
100   7/48
200   7/48
300   7/48
400   7/48

H 1
1   11/49

HOOSIER
702   6/51

HOP
2076   2/59

HOPPEROO
1   7/59

HORACE HEIDT
100   7/49

1005   8/49
1017   12/49
1018   2/50
1028   4/50
1050   8/50
1053   11/50
1060   9/51

HORIZON
706   9/53

HOROSCOPE
1001   7/52
1004   10/52

HORRIBLE
1   5/53

HOT
1   8/59

HOUSE OF
     BEAUTY
111   3/59

HOWARD
501   6/46

HRS
1003   8/45
1007   11/45
1015   1/46
1016   3/46
1019   2/48

HUB
3000   12/45
3001   1/46
3007   4/46
3015   5/46
3019   6/46
3029   7/46
3030   9/46
3032   10/46
3033   11/46
3045   7/48

5001   12/45
5002   1/46

HUB
501   8/53
502   10/53

1105   12/53
1107   4/54

HUBER
1005   11/57

HUCKSTERS
1002   3/47
1003   6/47
1009   2/48

HUDSON
519   4/49

HUDSON
1001   10/55
1007   3/56
1012   9/56

HULL
711   11/55
712   2/56
713   3/56
715   5/56
725   8/57

2025   7/56

HUNT
SEE ABC

HURRICANE					
100	11/58	5179	3/52	5444	6/57
101	5/59	5181	4/52	5454	7/57
		5182	5/52	5463	9/57
		5194	6/52	5469	10/57
HUSH		5195	7/52	5476	11/57
1000	9/58	5199	8/52	5483	12/57
		5202	9/52	5485	1/58
		5204	10/52	5491	2/58
		5208	11/52	5500	3/58
HUT		5210	12/52	5515	4/58
4401	1/58	5215	1/53	5519	5/58
4407	3/58	5229	3/53	5526	6/58
		5235	5/53	5529	7/58
		5237	6/53	5537	8/58
HY-TONE		5241	7/53	5541	9/58
32	3/48	5244	8/53	5549	10/58
		5248	9/53	5554	12/58
		5253	10/53	5562	1/59
		5258	11/53	5570	2/59
IGLOO		5263	1/54	5573	3/59
1003	12/59	5270	2/54	5585	4/59
		5274	3/54	5587	5/59
		5280	4/54	5591	6/59
IMPALA		5281	5/54	5602	7/59
203	7/59	5284	6/54	5610	8/59
		5292	7/54	5621	9/59
		5298	8/54	5626	10/59
IMPERIAL		5302	9/54	5632	11/59
329	1/49	5310	10/54	5633	12/59
395	1/50	5318	11/54	----------	
636	8/53	5325	1/55	7003	11/54
----------		5332	2/55	----------	
4001	8/48	5342	3/55	8019	1/48
----------		5348	4/55	8024	2/48
5013	1/48	5353	6/55	8040	8/48
5016	2/48	5356	7/55	8045	1/49
5019	3/48	5362	8/55	8047	2/49
5030	9/48	5364	10/55	8056	7/49
5032	1/49	5369	11/55	8065	11/49
5036	3/49	5370	12/55	8074	1/50
5040	6/49	5372	1/56	8081	6/50
5058	1/50	5379	2/56	8089	8/50
5064	3/50	5382	3/56	8104	3/51
5065	4/50	5389	4/56	8106	5/51
5072	5/50	5390	5/56	8123	9/51
5082	7/50	5392	6/56	8134	12/51
5089	8/50	5396	7/56	8144	3/52
5099	9/50	5399	8/56	8147	5/52
5102	10/50	5405	9/56	8157	7/52
5109	1/51	5410	10/56	8163	9/52
5114	2/51	5412	11/56	8167	11/52
5122	5/51	5422	1/57	8180	1/53
5132	7/51	5424	2/57	8181	2/53
5145	8/51	5432	3/57	8186	4/53
5153	10/51	5435	4/57	8188	5/53
5165	1/52	5442	5/57	8193	6/53
5167	2/52				

JAB
101   10/55
103   7/56

JACK BEE
1001   6/59
1003   8/59

JACKPOT
SEE CHALLENGE

JADE
SEE CASTLE

JAGUAR
202   4/54

3001   3/54
3004   4/54
3006   9/54
3007   11/54
3016   10/55
3028   2/59

JALO
101   10/56
102   11/56
----
201   3/58
202   6/58

JAMBOREE
SEE REPUBLIC

JAMBOREE
900   3/45
902   7/45
905   10/45
907   1/46
910   7/47

1001   7/49

JAMIE
SEE GUYDEN

JAMISON
5263   6/52

JAN
SEE JUBILEE

JAN
72249   8/49

JAN-D
0231   4/58

JANE
SEE JUBILEE

JANET
201   11/59

J & S
1602   11/57
1603   9/58

1652   2/57
1660   3/57

1701   6/59

1765   12/56

JAR
101   12/58
105   5/59

JARLAND
501   12/58

JARO
77002   8/59
77005   9/59
77007   10/59
77010   11/59

JAX
SEE CASTLE

JAXON
502   4/57
503   5/57
504   8/57

JAY
11   6/58
----
59   4/59
----
510   7/57

JAY BO
100   5/59

JAY DEE
SEE BEACON

JAY JAY
145   8/55
147   11/55
176   7/57
181   11/57
194   12/58
199   12/59

JAY SCOTT
1001   6/58

JAZZ LTD
201   6/49
----
401   6/49

JAZZ MAN
1   10/49
33   7/50

JAZZ RECORDS
1005   6/46
1011   5/47

JB
1003   6/57

J.C.D.
101   4/59
102   6/59
103   7/59
104   8/59

J.D.S.
5002   8/59
5003   10/59

JEAN
0001   10/58

JEB
3001   9/51
3017   5/52

JEFF
800   6/59

JEM
412   7/55
----
855   3/55

JESMA
463   7/51

JESTER
2   12/55

1002   8/56

2033   5/59

JET
501   2/58

1434   12/57

(FAN)
101   3/56
102   4/56

1928   7/56

JEWEL
SEE GEM

JEWEL
104   4/59
----
623   5/59

JIMSKAP
909   11/59

JIN
109   3/59

JM
1   7/59

JO-Z
SEE JUBILEE

JOB
114   5/58

J.O.B.
121   7/52

1007   7/52
1009   2/53
1010   3/53
1012   5/53
1014   7/53
1015   9/53

1100   11/53
1102   5/54
1104   6/54
1105   8/54
1107   6/55
1111   3/57

JODI
4103   4/59

JOE DAVIS
SEE BEACON

JOHNSON
105   12/57

JOLLY
102   9/50

JOLT
331   8/58
332   10/58

JON
4025   6/59

JONES
1001   7/58
1002   8/58

JOPZ
201   8/56
----
501   12/56
----
712   7/57

1001   9/57

JORRY
1734   12/57

JOSIE
SEE JUBILEE

JOTA
4000   12/59

JOURNAL
901   10/59

3533   7/58
3552   8/58

JOY
101   12/55
----
222   5/58
223   11/58

JOY CON'T		5106	12/52	5318	3/58
224	12/58	5108	1/53	5321	4/58
226	1/59	5109	2/53	5325	5/58
228	2/59	5113	3/53	5328	6/58
229	4/59	5115	4/53	5332	7/58
232	6/59	5117	5/53	5336	8/58
233	7/59	5120	6/53	5338	9/58
234	9/59	5122	7/53	5340	10/58
236	12/59	5125	9/53	5344	11/58
---------		5128	10/53	5354	12/58
1237	2/57	5131	12/53	5356	1/59
1240	5/57	5134	1/54	5358	2/59
		5135	2/54	5365	3/59
		5138	3/54	5370	4/59
JOYCE		5139	4/54	5372	5/59
1013	9/55	5141	5/54	5373	7/59
		5146	6/54	5375	8/59
		5154	7/54	---------	
JUBILEE		5159	10/54	6000	2/52
3003	1/51	5170	11/54	6002	4/52
---------		5174	12/54	6006	6/52
3501	10/47	5177	1/55	6009	7/52
3504	11/47	5180	2/55	6010	8/52
3508	6/48	5183	3/55	6018	9/52
---------		5189	4/55	6019	10/52
4005	8/50	5197	5/55	6020	11/52
4011	10/50	5203	6/55	6026	12/52
4013	11/50	5204	7/55	6027	1/53
4016	1/51	5209	8/55	6028	2/53
4025	3/51	5215	9/55	6033	4/53
4027	4/51	5218	10/55	6041	5/53
4040	6/51	5222	11/55	6044	7/53
---------		5227	12/55	6045	8/53
5000	10/48	5231	1/56	6052	11/53
5001	11/48	5234	2/56	6059	3/54
5002	1/49	5239	3/56	---------	
5004	4/49	5240	4/56	6000	9/59
5008	7/49	5245	5/56	6002	11/59
5009	8/49	5252	7/56	---------	
5018	2/50	5253	9/56	9000	5/53
5025	3/50	5257	10/56	9003	3/54
5026	5/50	5259	11/56	---------	
5029	6/50	5263	12/56	**(JO-Z)**	
5031	9/50	5266	1/57	**(JOSIE)**	
5037	10/50	5272	2/57	760	4/54
5042	11/50	5274	3/57	767	9/54
5051	1/51	5278	4/57	773	2/55
5056	6/51	5283	5/57	774	3/55
5060	9/51	5286	6/57	775	4/55
5070	12/51	5290	7/57	778	7/55
5073	3/52	5293	8/57	784	10/55
5080	4/52	5294	9/57	786	11/55
5083	6/52	5300	10/57	787	12/55
5091	8/52	5305	11/57	788	2/56
5093	9/52	5309	12/57	792	3/56
5098	11/52	5315	2/58	793	5/56

JUBILEE CON'T
(JOSIE)
798   6/56
802   8/56
803   10/56
805   11/56
808   12/56
810   2/57
814   4/57
818   5/57
821   7/57
822   8/57
825   12/57
831   1/58
832   2/58
834   3/58
836   4/58
837   5/58
839   6/58
841   7/58
842   8/58
844   10/58
847   11/58
848   12/58
854   1/59
857   2/59
858   3/59
859   4/59
863   5/59
864   6/59
866   7/59
867   8/59
872   10/59

(JAN)
100   3/58
101   5/58
102   7/58
(JANE)
103   10/58
106   1/59
107   5/59

(NATURAL)
5000   8/48

(PORT)
5000   5/57
5002   8/57
5006   10/58

70001   5/58
70003   7/58
70004   9/58
70005   10/58
70007   12/58

70010   4/59
70013   5/59
70014   8/59

JUDD
1001   8/58
1003   11/58
1006   12/58
1009   5/59
1013   7/59

JUDSON
003   5/58

JUKE BOX
SEE SPECIALTY

JUKE BOX
100   5/55
101   12/55
102   3/56
106   4/57
108   10/57

1001   11/54

JUNIOR
55   6/50

1006   3/50

JUNO
213   11/57

1013   6/53

JUPITER
1   6/57
2   7/57
----
210   4/57
211   5/57

JURY
3001

KADY
103   6/59

KAHI
120   5/59

KAHILL
1006   10/55
1013   9/56
1015   12/56
1024   2/57

KAISER
401   4/59
----
592   11/57

KALKO
2016   8/59

KANDY
104   12/56
111   10/57
125   10/59

KANGEROO
13   9/58
14   6/59
15   8/59
----
600   4/59

KANGEROO
1301   3/49

KAPP
100   6/54
102   7/54
104   8/54
105   9/54
106   10/54
108   1/55
111   2/55
112   3/55
113   4/55
115   6/55
116   7/55
120   9/55

KAPP CON'T		KAT		82108	12/59
129	1/56	119	10/59	----------	
138	2/56			(ANDEX)	
140	3/56			22102	9/59
143	4/56	KAWANA		22103	10/59
148	5/56	102	9/59	----------	
153	7/56			4006	2/58
154	8/56	KAY		4011	4/58
158	9/56	1001	6/58	4012	5/58
162	11/56			34022	7/58
165	12/56			4027	11/58
170	1/57	KAYO		4031	2/59
174	2/57	501	12/59	4033	3/59
176	3/57	----------		4034	4/59
180	4/57	927	9/58	34036	6/59
182	5/57			----------	
185	6/57			5001	10/57
191	7/57	KAY-Y		----------	
193	8/57	66780	12/57	(ENSIGN)	
196	11/57	66781	7/58	2009	11/58
206	12/57			2015	4/59
207	1/58			----------	
209	2/58	KCM		4014	5/58
213	3/58	3700	9/58	4019	6/58
217	4/58	3701	1/59	4021	7/58
219	5/58	3702	6/59	4030	1/59
226	6/58			4035	6/59
231	7/58			4037	7/59
233	8/58	KEE			
238	9/58	100	8/47	KELIT	
242	10/58			7033	8/58
249	11/58				
253	12/58	KEEN			
257	1/59	KEENE		KELLEY	
261	2/59	34013	9/57	105	4/59
270	4/59	34001	10/57		
278	5/59	4005	2/58	KEM	
284	6/59	4010	4/58	2700	5/49
288	7/59	4018	6/58	2701	7/49
294	8/59	----------		2705	3/50
302	9/59	2001	2/58	2706	6/50
303	10/59	32002	3/58	2711	3/52
		32004	4/58	2713	8/52
		2006	7/58	2714	10/52
KAPPA		2007	8/58	2719	12/52
108	11/48	2008	10/58	2720	3/53
115	8/49	2013	12/58	2722	4/53
119	12/49	2014	1/59	2723	5/53
207	5/58	2017	2/59	2727	7/53
----------		2020	5/59	2729	11/53
703	11/48	2023	6/59	2730	12/53
		----------		2731	2/54
KAREN		2101	8/59	2732	4/54
1005	9/59	82103	9/59	2733	7/54
		82106	11/59		

KEM CON'T

2736	2/55
2737	4/55
2739	7/55
2742	3/56
2743	2/57
2744	6/57
2753	11/58

KENT
SEE MODERN

KENT

5001	9/56

KENTUCKY

523	5/52
574	5/53
584	9/53
1522	3/52

KERNEL

002	5/57

KERRY

101	8/56
7711	5/58

KEY

501	4/55
503	5/55
506	8/55
507	11/55
509	2/56
510	3/56
513	8/56
516	10/56
517	1/57
575	5/57
1001	4/59
1061	4/59
1064	5/59
5710	7/57
5712	9/57

5718	11/57
5719	1/58
5801	3/58
5903	3/58

KEYBOARD

356	7/50
360	3/51
500	2/52

KEYNOTE

111	7/42
141	10/47
309	12/44
536	12/44
604	3/44
605	4/44
611	1/45
613	3/45
616	7/45
618	8/45
619	10/45
620	11/45
621	1/46
626	4/46
635	10/46
665	2/47
1202	5/44
1300	5/44
1302	6/44
1314	10/45
1316	11/45
1317	1/46
10001	10/47

KEYNOTE

110	11/55
1002	5/53
1204	5/59

KEYSTONE

102	7/49
632	4/50
1415	1/52
1500	4/50
1503	2/52
1600	4/49
1800	4/49
1900	4/49
2000	4/49
2100	4/49
5101	4/50
10001	4/50

KEYSTONE

666	12/58

KHOURY'S

644	12/54

KICKS

5-F	12/54
516	7/58

KIL-MAC

1412	9/59

KING

500	11/43
507	10/44
508	9/45
514	2/46
526	3/46
528	4/46
530	5/46
532	6/46
539	7/46
544	8/46
558	11/46
583	12/46

KING CON'T		1109	9/52	4218	4/48
586	1/47	1120	10/52	4220	5/48
606	2/47	1132	11/52	4229	6/48
612	3/47	1150	12/52	4231	7/48
623	5/47	1154	1/53	4249	10/48
639	6/47	1174	2/53	4255	11/48
660	8/47	1181	3/53	4263	12/48
665	9/47	1213	4/53	4264	1/49
668	11/47	1221	5/53	4283	3/49
676	12/47	1229	6/53	4292	4/49
689	1/48	1239	7/53	4296	6/49
694	2/48	1256	8/53	4303	7/49
695	3/48	1268	10/53	4309	8/49
712	4/48	1288	11/53	4311	9/49
714	5/48	1289	12/53	4315	10/49
719	6/48	1298	1/54	4321	11/49
723	7/48	1315	2/54	4326	12/49
735	9/48	1337	3/54	4337	1/50
737	10/48	1339	4/54	4339	2/50
739	11/48	1348	5/54	4343	3/50
749	1/49	1355	6/54	4353	4/50
777	2/49	1361	7/54	4358	5/50
778	5/49	1372	8/54	4373	6/50
788	6/49	1379	9/54	4377	7/50
792	7/49	1396	11/54	4388	8/50
804	8/49	1412	11/54	4393	9/50
809	9/49	1416	1/55	4405	10/50
811	10/49	1426	2/55	4409	11/50
821	11/49	1444	3/55	4422	12/50
837	12/49	1449	4/55	4424	1/51
840	2/50	1473	6/55	4427	2/51
847	3/50	1482	7/55	4429	3/51
855	4/50	1493	8/55	4450	5/51
859	6/50	1497	9/55	4456	6/51
876	7/50	1508	10/55	4476	8/51
893	8/50	---------		4482	11/51
901	9/50	(QUEEN)		4493	12/51
905	10/50	4108	2/46	4515	1/52
909	11/50	4110	3/46	4523	3/52
918	12/50	4113	4/46	4525	4/52
924	1/51	4115	5/46	4535	5/52
932	3/51	4119	6/46	4541	6/52
954	5/51	4122	7/46	4546	7/52
958	6/51	4126	8/46	4550	8/52
977	7/51	4135	9/46	4557	9/52
986	9/51	4147	11/46	4569	10/52
999	10/51	4162	3/47	4573	11/52
1001	11/51	4165	5/47	4583	12/52
1017	12/51	4171	6/47	4589	1/53
1038	1/52	(KING)		4608	2/53
1042	2/52	4175	8/47	4610	3/53
1057	3/52	4178	8/47	4616	4/53
1065	5/52	4196	11/47	4628	5/53
1076	6/52	4198	12/47	4630	6/53
1079	7/52	4200	1/48	4640	7/53
1088	8/52	4203	2/48	4656	8/53

KING CON'T

4661	9/53	5145	8/58	15214	12/52
4672	10/53	5147	9/58	15215	1/53
4683	11/53	5153	10/58	15220	2/53
4687	12/53	5159	11/58	----------	
4691	1/54	5163	12/58	(DELUXE)	
4699	2/54	5171	1/59	203	6/49
4702	3/54	5178	2/59	----------	
4703	4/54	5182	3/59	1001	6/45
4715	5/54	5196	4/59	1002	9/45
4718	6/54	5205	5/59	1003	11/45
4729	7/54	5209	6/59	1005	12/45
4730	8/54	5220	7/59	1007	1/46
4741	10/54	5238	8/59	1009	3/46
4755	12/54	5252	9/59	1025	6/46
4765	1/55	5266	10/59	1033	8/46
4770	2/55	5275	11/59	1045	11/46
4776	3/55	5310	12/59	1049	12/46
4788	4/55	----------		1057	1/47
4796	5/55	15000	4/49	1058	2/47
4802	6/55	15006	6/49	1063	3/47
4812	7/55	15007	7/49	1071	4/47
4819	8/55	15009	8/49	1076	5/47
4824	9/55	15017	9/49	1081	7/47
4827	10/55	15018	11/49	1086	8/47
4846	11/55	15023	12/49	1089	10/47
4860	12/55	15032	2/50	1120	11/47
4867	1/56	15040	4/50	1121	12/47
4883	2/56	15044	5/50	1145	2/48
4903	3/56	15045	6/50	1154	3/48
4909	4/56	15057	7/50	1157	4/48
4937	6/56	15060	8/50	1173	5/48
4943	7/56	15064	9/50	1176	6/48
4953	8/56	15072	10/50	1182	10/48
4960	9/56	15074	11/50	1184	11/48
4970	10/56	15090	12/50	1188	1/49
5000	11/56	15092	1/51	1192	3/49
5004	12/56	15093	2/51	1194	5/49
5005	1/57	15102	3/51	SEE REGAL	
5023	3/57	15106	4/51	----------	
5038	4/57	15107	5/51	2000	5/44
5048	5/57	15108	7/51	2004	6/45
5063	6/57	15114	9/51	----------	
5066	7/57	15126	10/51	2000	11/53
5072	8/57	15132	11/51	2006	12/53
5074	9/57	15145	12/51	2008	1/54
5082	10/57	15154	1/52	2018	2/54
5088	11/57	15161	2/52	2019	3/54
5094	12/57	15166	3/52	2020	4/54
5104	1/58	15178	4/52	2022	8/54
5115	2/58	15182	5/52	----------	
5120	3/58	15188	6/52	3000	5/45
5128	4/58	15189	7/52	3001	7/45
5132	5/58	15196	8/52	3005	10/45
5140	6/58	15200	9/52	----------	
5144	7/58	15201	10/52	3177	7/48
		15203	11/52	3192	10/48

KING CON'T
DELUXE)

3196	11/48	6047	4/54	12002	1/51
3200	1/49	6051	5/54	12016	2/51
3207	2/49	6055	6/54	12028	4/51
3209	3/49	6056	8/54	12034	6/51
3213	5/49	6059	9/54	12036	7/51
3226	6/49	6063	11/54	12045	9/51
3228	8/49	6066	12/54	12056	2/52

SEE REGAL

		6080	2/55	12059	3/52
3300	10/49	6083	4/55	12065	4/52
3301	2/50	6090	6/55	12070	5/52
3302	4/50	6091	12/55	12082	6/52
3303	6/50	6093	3/56	12085	7/52
3304	9/50	6094	4/56	12090	8/52
3309	11/50	6095	6/56	12098	9/52
3311	1/51	6096	7/56	12101	10/52
3312	3/51	6097	9/56	12108	11/52
3315	4/51	6099	12/56	12114	12/52
3316	5/51	6107	2/57	12115	2/53
3318	7/51	6115	3/57	12118	3/53
3320	9/51	6121	4/57	12127	5/53
3321	1/52	6129	5/57	12130	6/53
3323	3/52	6138	6/57	12135	7/53
		6140	7/57	12141	8/53
5001	3/44	6144	8/57	12142	9/53
5003	4/44	6145	9/57	12150	10/53
5007	7/44	6151	10/57	12151	11/53
5009	2/45	6152	11/57	12159	12/53
5011	3/46	6153	12/57	12163	1/54
5012	5/46	6159	2/58	12165	2/54
5013	6/46	6162	4/58	12171	3/54
5015	7/46	6163	5/58	12175	4/54
5019	1/47	6166	6/58	12180	5/54
5025	2/47	6167	7/58	12186	6/54
5027	3/47	6170	8/58	12190	7/54
5035	5/47	6172	9/58	12191	8/54
5038	1/48	6176	10/58	12200	10/54
5039	2/48	6180	12/58	12202	12/54
5040	3/48	6181	2/59	12206	1/55
5043	6/48	6182	3/59	12209	2/55
5047	10/48	6185	4/59	12215	3/55
5051	12/48	6186	7/59	12227	7/55
5057	1/49			12239	10/55

SEE REGAL

		9152	8/48	12244	11/55
				12245	12/55
6000	3/47	(FEDERAL)		12249	1/56
6002	5/47			12255	2/56
		10002	3/51	12256	3/56
6018	10/53	10005	4/51	12260	4/56
6019	11/53	10012	5/51	12267	5/56
6023	12/53	10016	6/51	12272	6/56
6027	1/54	10021	7/51	12275	7/56
6036	2/54	10024	9/51	12277	8/56
6040	3/54	10029	10/51	12278	9/56
		10030	12/51	12280	10/56
				12289	1/57
		12001	12/50	12293	4/57

KING CON'T
FEDERAL

12295	5/57
12300	7/57
12304	8/57
12306	9/57
12309	10/57
12311	11/57
12312	12/57
12317	2/58
12320	3/58
12324	4/58
12327	5/58
12331	7/58
12334	9/58
12337	10/58
12338	11/58
12342	12/58
12346	1/59
12347	2/59
12349	3/49
12352	4/59
12354	5/59
12357	6/59
12360	7/59
12362	8/59
12366	9/59
12368	11/59

14001	7/51
14002	9/51
14003	5/52
14004	7/52

(GLORY)

4003	12/52
4011	3/53
4014	7/53

(ROCKIN')

503	12/52
506	3/53
510	5/53
514	8/53

KING JAZZ

141	6/46
143	5/48

KING SOLOMON
SEE SAVOY

KINGSPORT

109	1/53

KIP

400	3/59

KISMET

101	8/43
104	9/43

KIT

883	3/56

KLICK

1001	2/52
1006	3/55

1604	9/55
1621	9/58

KLIFF

100	6/58

KLIK

305	6/58

7805	12/57

7905	2/58

8205	4/58

8405	7/58

KLIX

001	4/58

KLONDIKE

1010	2/59

KNICK

1713	5/58
1714	9/58

KNIGHT
SEE IMPERIAL

KNIGHT

2007	4/50

KNOTTY

101	8/53

5581	10/55

5642	6/56

KNOX

101	7/59

201	8/59

KOBB

1501	3/58

KODIAK

1	8/59

KOOL

1001	4/59
1002	6/59

KRANZ

601	6/48

1014	1/48
1023	5/48

KRC
SEE ATLANTIC
SEE ACE

KRYSLAR

5571	3/55

9001	10/54

K-SON

7771	9/57

KUDO

664	6/58

LA BONITA	**L & C**	**LAUREL-LI**
400 2/48	550 1/56	401 9/59

LABEL	**LAR**	**LAURIE**
2020 3/59	102 5/59	3013 4/58
		3015 7/58
		3021 11/58
LAD	**LARIAT**	3022 12/58
0027 4/59	1051 10/51	3023 1/59
	----------	3024 3/59
	1101 4/52	3028 5/59
LAFF	----------	3033 8/59
505 10/47	1201 10/52	3038 9/59
	1203 12/52	3041 11/59
		3044 12/59
LAITIME		----------
999 10/58	**LARK**	**(ANDIE)**
	SEE DEL FI	5013 11/59

LAMAAR STAR	**LARK**	**LEADER**
501 9/45	1001 9/47	100 11/53

LAMB	**LARO**	**LE CAM**
10-105 9/48	582 6/58	701 5/59
		706 11/59

LAMP	**LARRY**	**LEDA**
SEE ALADDIN	801 8/59	2001 1/50

LAMPLIGHTER	**LASALLE**	**LEE**
101 4/46	501 3/57	100 6/58
110 9/46		----------
		502 6/56
	LAS VEGAS	503 1/57
LANCE	1401 8/59	504 9/58
125 9/57		----------
		1001 11/58
	LATIN AMERICAN	1002 4/59
LANCER	44 1/50	1003 7/59
104 3/59		1004 11/59
105 9/59		

LANE	**LAUREL**	**LEE**
501 4/58	1 1/56	202 2/50
	----------	----------
	1010 11/59	8021 2/50
LANIER		----------
001 9/58	**LAUREL**	1002 2/48
	7000 6/49	

LANJO
6845   7/59

LEEDS
779	11/58
780	1/59
782	2/59

LEGEND
101	12/57
102	1/59

LENA
1001	1/59

LENARD
1588	5/58

LENOX
500	9/48
510	11/48
514	4/49
531	12/49

LEO
401	6/53
784	7/59
1824	5/57

LEO'S
2005	5/59
5974	8/59

LESLIE
918	7/49

LEWIS
111	10/50

LEX
0316	11/58

LEXINGTON
100	8/58

LHS
1002	10/57

LIBERTY
1	12/45
201	12/49
3001	11/48
4567	2/46

LIBERTY
55001	4/55
55003	5/55
55005	7/55
55006	10/55
55007	11/55
55008	12/55
55009	2/56
55019	3/56
55020	5/56
55021	6/56
55022	7/56
55026	8/56
55034	10/56
55040	11/56
55043	12/56
55050	1/57
55052	2/57
55055	3/57
55059	4/57
55066	5/57
55073	6/57
55083	7/57
55093	8/57
55102	9/57
55107	11/57
55116	12/57
55119	1/58
55124	2/58
55126	3/58
55136	4/58
55138	6/58
55144	7/58
55148	8/58
55156	9/58
55159	10/58
55168	11/58
55169	12/58
55170	1/59
55177	2/59
55180	3/59
55193	4/59

55194	6/59
55201	7/59
55206	8/59
55210	9/59
55214	10/59
55215	11/59
55226	12/59

(DOLPHIN)
1	2/59

(DOLTON)
2	5/59
4	6/59
10	11/59
611	9/59

(FREEDOM)
44001	9/58
44002	10/58
44003	11/58
44005	1/59
44006	2/59
44008	3/59
44009	4/59
44013	5/59
44015	6/59
44016	7/59
44021	8/59
44024	10/59
44025	12/59

LIBERTY BELL
9004	7/54
9008	7/56
9009	10/56
9011	1/57
9012	2/57
9015	4/57
9016	5/57
9017	6/57
9014	7/57
9020	10/57
1078	1/56

LIDO
101	2/50
500	10/56
600	6/59
1150	2/50

LIFE
5   3/58

LIFE
1000   8/48
1001   2/50
1003   7/50
1011   3/52

52822   6/48

LIGHT HOUSE
401   4/59

LIGHTNING
104   6/55
105   8/55
111   11/55
----
301   8/55

LIMELIGHT
SEE MERCURY

LIN
1005   10/54
1012   7/55
1014   8/55
1015   10/55
1016   12/55

1051   2/54

2000   7/59

5000   7/55
5001   1/56
5012   6/58
5015   7/58
5019   3/59
5023   10/59

LINA
004   9/49
031   6/50

1503   6/50

LINCO
1313   5/59

LINCOLN
240   4/50
----
514   12/49
515   2/50
----
816   2/50

LINDA
107   7/57
109   6/58

1000   10/59

LINDY
741   11/58

1124   4/59

LINWOOD
502   12/55

LISSEN
105   5/47

1038   6/47
1039   8/47
1040   9/47
1041   10/47

LISTEN
1430   6/52
1433   9/52
1450   11/52

LLOYDS
SEE APOLLO

LOED
094   8/59

2005   9/58

LOGAN
3103   12/58
3104   1/59
3106   2/59
3107   3/59
3111   4/59
3112   5/59
3117   7/59

LOGUE
806   10/57

LONDON
110   12/47
142   1/48
187   2/48
196   3/48
202   4/48
206   5/48
223   6/48
236   7/48
275   8/48
281   9/48
309   10/48
353   11/48
367   1/49
410   2/49
413   3/49
414   4/49
433   5/49
453   6/49
457   7/49
500   8/49
513   10/49
529   11/49
603   12/49
609   1/50
619   2/50
630   3/50
659   4/50
677   5/50
716   6/50
752   7/50
762   8/50
769   9/50
782   10/50
795   11/50
873   12/50
879   1/51
919   2/51
978   3/51
994   4/51
1027   5/51
1031   6/51

LONDON CON'T					
1084	7/51	1712	1/57	30017	7/50
1086	8/51	1731	4/57		
1130	11/51	1735	5/57		
1134	12/51	1749	6/57	LONE STAR	
1141	1/52	1750	7/57	101	10/47
1180	2/52	1756	8/57	103	11/47
1183	3/52	1757	9/57	---------	
1192	4/52	1770	11/57	4113	12/47
1200	5/52	1779	12/57		
1223	6/52	1788	2/58		
1234	7/52	1794	3/58	LONGHORN	
1247	8/52	1797	4/58	501	2/57
1254	9/52	1800	5/58	504	12/57
1261	10/52	1811	6/58		
1274	11/52	1813	7/58		
1278	12/52	1827	9/58	LOOK	
1282	1/53	1834	10/58	102	5/54
1295	2/53	1840	11/58	104	5/55
1300	3/53	1841	12/58	108	3/56
1328	4/53	1852	1/59	---------	
1342	5/53	1857	2/59	1000	10/57
1357	7/53	1860	3/59		
1371	9/53	1864	4/59		
1372	10/53	1870	5/59	LOOP	
1386	11/53	1871	6/59	806	11/49
1389	12/53	1877	8/59	---------	
1433	1/54	1888	11/59	903	9/49
1448	2/54	1895	12/59		
1455	5/54	---------			
1482	6/54	10013	5/48	LORAY	
1486	7/54	10034	8/48	500	9/52
1491	8/54	10040	11/48		
1495	9/54	10095	6/49		
1501	10/54	---------		LOTUS	
1502	11/54	11183	3/52	1	8/50
1523	1/55	11360	11/52		
1534	2/55	11390	12/52		
1550	3/55	---------		LOVE	
1554	4/55	12001	5/48	5001	4/58
1572	5/55	12007	11/48	5004	8/58
1578	6/55	12138	7/52	5014	11/58
1584	7/55	---------		5018	2/59
1585	8/55	16001	10/49	5020	4/59
1598	9/55	16014	1/50	5022	6/59
1605	10/55	16019	3/50	5023	7/59
1620	12/55	16023	5/50		
1629	1/56	16026	6/50		
1637	2/56	16056	2/51	LOWE	
1645	3/56	---------		101	12/59
1659	5/56	17000	9/49		
1671	6/56	17008	3/50		
1675	7/56	17011	5/50	LOWERY	
1796	9/56	---------		1001	12/53
1698	10/56	20021	2/51	1008	8/54
1711	12/56	---------			
		30065	5/50		

LOYAL	
111	2/55

LU	
501	12/57
502	3/58
506	6/59
---	---
5000	10/57

LUCKY	
0001	8/58
0005	7/59
0006	9/59
---	---
004	5/54
---	---
7-11-2	10/48
7-11-3	11/48
7-11-4	1/49
7-11-6	2/49
---	---
711-8	
---	---
7-1002	10/50
---	---
1000	1/52
1004	4/52
1006	7/54

LUCKY SEVEN	
101	1/59
102	4/59

LUCKY STAR	
4410	6/52

LUCKY SUN	
100	5/59

LUDWIG	
1007	10/58

LUMMTONE	
101	9/59

LUNA	
10-101	6/54

LUNAR	
519	5/59

LUNIVERSAL	
101	7/56
102	10/56
103	2/57
---	---
(ELDORADO)	
501	11/56
504	1/57
505	2/57
508	5/57

LYRIC	
101	1/58
103	3/58

MACGREGOR	
793	6/57
---	---
1003	2/50
1016	7/50
1021	11/50
1023	3/51
1025	11/51
1026	3/52
1035	4/54

MACY'S	
101	8/49
109	11/49
112	12/49
116	2/50
120	4/50
130	7/50
141	8/50
144	9/50
---	---
1000	3/50
---	---
5000	12/49
5004	1/50
5005	4/50
5006	6/50
5007	7/50

MAD	
1007	8/58
---	---
1207	5/58

MADISON	
102	7/58
104	9/58
109	1/59
110	3/59
117	6/59
118	8/59
121	9/59
---	---
321	6/56
---	---
822	2/55
---	---
1492	7/55

MAESTRO	
317	10/55
---	---
702	6/46
---	---
3397	5/51

MAGIC	
001	4/49
---	---
11	5/51
13	2/54
---	---
2-100	4/50
---	---
1005	2/49
---	---
4232	5/50

MAGNOLIA	
1001	4/49
1009	6/49
1011	8/49
1018	1/50

MAINE	
6000	4/59

MAINLINE	
101	3/57

MAIN STEM	
702	4/49

MAJAR
25   8/54
----
131   9/54
135   11/54
136   12/54
138   3/55
143   4/55

MAJESTIC
SEE VARSITY

MAJESTIC
1358   11/58

2196   3/59

2984   2/59

7581   5/58

MAJOR
144   6/51

MAJOR
1001   9/58
1004   12/58

MAJORETTE
102   9/53

MALA
400   7/59
404   9/59
408   10/59
411   12/59

MAMBO
105   7/55
109   9/55

M&B
101   4/58

M&J
1   11/55
5   6/58

115   10/56

2-1   11/56

3-2   11/56

M&M
2020   1/56

3031   1/56

MANHATTEN
502   5/56
507   9/58
----
612   5/55

MANHATTEN
2003   11/48

MANNING
5262   8/59

MANOR
SEE REGIS

MANSFIELD
604   5/56
611   5/57

MANVELLO
4954   7/54

MARATHON
182   11/59
----
503   7/56

1014   11/51

MARCEL
107   12/58

MARDI-GRAS
1002   12/54
1014   10/55

1020   5/56
1023   11/56
1027   3/57

MARGUEE
700   3/59

MARILYN
804   12/56

MARK
103   2/57
104   5/57
106   8/57
107   9/57
110   12/57
112   1/58
116   3/58
122   5/58
126   7/58
129   8/58
137   10/58
140   11/58
141   2/59

1041   12/56
1051   5/57

4056   5/58

MARKEE
MAR-KEE
100   8/47

MARK 56
801   11/58

MARK-X
SEE ROULETTE

MARLBORO
1001   12/59

MARLENE
102   6/57
----
333   5/58

MARLINDA
1526   8/59

MARQUEE
1018   6/55
1023   9/55
1031   10/55
1033   2/56

MARS
200   8/52
----
400   11/52
----
500   11/53
----
600   3/53
----
800   8/53

1001   10/53
1003   11/53
1005   5/54
1008   1/56

MARS
1010   9/46

MARTERRY
SEE ARISTOCRAT

MARTINIQUE
101   5/58
----
400   3/59

MARTONY
100   5/49

MARVEL
MAR-VEL
111   3/56
----
151   3/55
----
230   3/56
----
301   2/54
----

355   8/56
----
505   11/53
----
600   9/57
----
750   7/54
753   11/58
----
781   7/55
----
820   11/54
----
900   7/52
901   9/53
902   5/56
----
950   9/53
952   2/55
953   5/56

1000   6/57
1002   9/57

1201   6/57

1350   6/57

1400   8/58

1500   11/58

10501   9/49
10502   1/52
10505   4/53
10508   8/57

MARVELTONE
713   2/58

MARY HOWARD
123   7/47
128   10/47

MASCOT
123   12/59

MASQUERADE
803   9/57

10302   5/55

22459   4/58

56001   8/56

MASTER
SEE MIRACLE

MASTER
363   6/53
367   8/53
371   11/53
373   6/54
374   11/54
375   1/55
377   3/55

MASTER SOUND
1005   6/59

MASTERTONE
75-13   11/46

75-100-1
          12/50

MAUNAY
101   8/49
102   12/49
103   11/50
104   7/51
105   12/53

MAYFAIR
411   8/57
421   4/58

MAY FAIR
5001   12/49

MAYFLOWER
16   8/59
17   11/59

MAYHAMS
1598   6/58

MAYJOE
2001   7/53

MAZE
1017   2/56

MCI
1001   1/56
1003   5/56
1005   5/58

MGM
333   8/59
----
777   1/59

MDA
852   11/59

MECCA
101   7/47
104   1/48

MECCA
101   4/53
106   6/53

MECCA
2422   8/59

2500   8/59

MEDALION
501   9/59

MEDALION
4054   6/52

MEDIA
1008   4/55
1009   5/55
1010   6/55
1013   7/55
1014   9/55
1016   10/55
1018   11/55

1019   12/55
1021   2/56

MEDLEY
133   6/54

MELBA
102   2/56
103   5/56
106   7/56
119   5/57

MELDEAN
200   6/57

MELFORD
253   8/49
255   12/49

MELLO
4101   3/56

MELLO-STRAIN
100   3/46
102   11/46
108   7/47
114   6/49
117   7/50

MELMAR
1041   5/54

MELODISC
101   6/45
107   8/45
110   9/45
111   1/46
116   3/46
----
502   7/46

1001   2/46
1012   8/46

MELODY
5002   4/59

MELODY GUY
101   10/53

MELODY TRAIL
187   6/48
205   7/48
211   4/49
218   7/49

MELODYTUNE
11   3/46

MEL-O-TONE
1135   10/56

3433   4/57

MEMO
110   4/48

1033   9/45
1092   11/45
1098   1/46
1135   2/46

3001   4/48

5001   6/46

5100   3/48

7001   3/48

9109   3/48

MEMO
17984   10/59

MENAGERIE
101   3/49

MERCER
1950   10/50
1951   11/50
1953   12/50
1956   2/51
1965   5/51
1966   9/51

MERCURY					
2001	11/45	5301	6/49	6057	10/47
2010	12/45	5310	7/49	6066	11/47
2033	1/46	5315	8/49	6074	1/48
2039	2/46	5318	9/49	6093	2/48
2060	3/46	5322	10/49	6098	4/48
2071	4/46	5334	11/49	6104	5/48
2075	5/46	5347	12/49	6110	6/48
--------		5360	1/50	6116	7/48
		5361	2/50	6124	8/48
3001	3/46	5377	3/50	6139	9/48
3003	4/46	5385	4/50	6141	10/48
3007	5/46	5421	5/50	6148	11/48
3017	6/46	5441	6/50	6153	1/49
3025	7/46	5445	7/50	6167	3/49
3026	8/46	5458	8/50	6175	4/49
3028	9/46	5480	9/50	6189	5/49
3031	10/46	5500	10/50	6192	6/49
3043	11/46	5534	11/50	6200	7/49
3046	12/46	5555	12/50	6209	9/49
3050	1/47	5567	1/51	6213	10/49
3055	2/47	5585	2/51	6216	11/49
3057	3/47	5606	3/51	6221	12/49
3059	4/47	5624	4/51	6224	1/50
3061	5/47	5645	5/51	6233	2/50
3063	6/47	5656	6/51	6241	3/50
3064	7/47	5676	7/51	6246	4/50
3069	9/47	5687	8/51	6252	5/50
3072	11/47	5707	9/51	6263	6/50
--------		5726	10/51	6264	8/50
5000	9/46	5736	11/51	6279	10/50
5003	10/46	5764	12/51	6288	11/50
5006	11/46	5772	1/52	6301	2/51
5012	1/47	5780	2/52	6310	3/51
5035	3/47	5798	3/52	6325	4/51
5048	4/47	5832	4/52	6326	6/51
5049	5/47	5851	5/52	6347	7/51
5054	6/47	5866	6/52	6353	8/51
5055	7/47	5881	7/52	6358	10/51
5062	8/47	5893	8/52	6362	11/51
5064	10/47	5902	9/52	6370	1/52
5073	11/47	5912	10/52	6379	3/52
5084	12/47	--------		6392	4/52
5093	1/48	6004	4/46	6399	6/52
5109	2/48	6005	5/46	6405	7/52
5126	4/48	6009	6/46	6410	8/52
5133	5/48	6011	8/46	6414	9/52
5146	6/48	6013	9/46	6419	10/52
5172	8/48	6015	10/46	--------	
5190	10/48	6023	11/46	8002	3/46
5210	11/48	6025	12/46	8003	4/46
5225	12/48	6031	1/47	8006	5/46
5229	1/49	6034	3/47	8010	6/46
5245	2/49	6044	5/47	8012	7/46
5263	3/49	6048	6/47	8014	8/46
5280	4/49	6052	8/47	8018	9/46
5281	5/49	6054	9/47	8020	10/46

MERCURY
CON'T

8027	11/46	8909	11/49	70426	8/54
8029	1/47	8911	1/50	70443	9/54
8030	2/47	8917	4/50	70456	10/54
8035	4/47	8929	2/51	70482	11/54
8037	5/47	8930	3/51	70516	12/54
8045	7/47	8939	5/51	70528	1/55
8050	10/47	8945	6/51	70544	2/55
8060	11/47	8948	7/51	70573	3/55
8065	12/47	8950	8/51	70600	4/55
8067	1/48	8952	9/51	70630	5/55
8075	3/48	8954	10/51	70647	6/55
8078	4/48	8964	3/52	70669	7/55
8083	5/48	8996	8/52	70676	8/55
8088	6/48	--------		70699	9/55
8092	7/48	11025	1/50	70713	10/55
8098	8/48	11058	2/51	70743	11/55
8108	10/48	11076	5/51	70753	12/55
8111	11/48	11081	6/51	70774	1/56
8113	12/48	11082	8/51	70790	2/56
8116	1/49	11083	10/51	70818	3/56
8122	2/49	11087	3/52	70850	4/56
8124	3/49	11089	7/52	70872	5/56
8129	4/49	11090	8/52	70879	6/56
8135	5/49	11091	12/52	70910	7/56
8146	7/49	11095	1/53	70934	8/56
8150	8/49	11100	8/53	70942	9/56
8153	10/49	11101	1/54	70975	10/56
8154	11/49	--------		70989	11/56
8163	2/50	15001	11/47	71008	12/56
8168	4/50	15002	2/48	71028	1/57
8181	5/50	15003	8/48	71050	2/57
8183	7/50	--------		71072	3/57
8192	8/50	70000	10/45	71084	4/57
8207	12/50	--------		71101	5/57
8209	1/51	70003	10/52	71128	6/57
8211	2/51	70004	11/52	71140	7/57
8232	3/51	70045	12/52	71169	8/57
8233	5/51	70074	1/53	71180	9/57
8240	6/51	70090	2/53	71203	10/57
8244	7/51	70114	3/53	71223	11/57
8253	9/51	70127	4/53	71262	1/58
8254	10/51	70153	5/53	71279	2/58
8257	11/51	70170	6/53	71291	3/58
8259	12/51	70189	7/53	71298	4/58
8263	1/52	70211	7/53	71315	5/58
8272	3/52	70212	9/53	71331	6/58
8274	4/52	70234	10/53	71343	7/58
8277	5/52	70256	11/53	71346	8/58
8280	6/52	70277	12/53	71355	9/58
8284	7/52	70287	1/54	71369	10/58
8289	8/52	70317	2/54	71382	11/58
8298	10/52	70339	3/54	71390	12/58
--------		70346	4/54	71404	1/59
8906	1/49	70366	5/54	71414	2/59
		70391	6/54	71427	3/59
		70409	7/54	71449	4/59

MERCURY
CON'T

71754	5/59
71470	6/59
71480	7/59
71486	8/59
71510	9/59
71519	10/59
71534	11/59
71561	12/59

89000	8/52
89001	9/52
89011	11/52
89018	1/53
89025	2/53
89031	3/53
89036	4/53
89042	5/53
89056	6/53
89061	7/53

SEE CLEF

(EMARCY)

16000	5/54
16008	6/54
16011	7/54
16015	8/54

(LIMELIGHT)

3001	3/58
3004	4/58

(WING)

90000	6/55
90008	7/55
90013	8/55
90016	9/55
90027	10/55
90034	11/55
90044	12/559
90045	1/56
90054	2/56
90058	3/56
90067	4/56
90074	5/56
90078	6/56
90082	7/56

MERCY BABY

501	12/58
502	6/59

MERIDEN

8934	12/54

MERIDIAN

4778	7/59

MERIT

300	7/49
305	6/51

1101	11/55

MARLENE

333	5/58

MET

1002	11/53
1005	3/54

MET TEMPO

92	8/53

METEOR
SEE MODERN

METRO
SEE MGM

METRO
SEE MILTONE

METROPOLITAN

20-01	7/48
20-02	10/49

100	7/47

METROTONE

1000	10/47
1011	3/48

MGM

10001	2/47
10005	3/47
10011	4/47
10019	5/47
10036	6/47
10044	7/47
10050	8/47
10070	9/47
10071	10/47
10102	11/47
10108	12/47
10128	1/48
10142	2/48
10151	3/48
10171	4/48
10185	5/48
10206	6/48
10223	7/48
10241	8/48
10271	9/48
10274	10/48
10316	12/48
10331	1/49
10354	2/49
10374	3/49
10381	4/49
10415	5/49
10440	6/49
10460	7/49
10490	8/49
10506	9/49
10514	10/49
10564	11/49
10570	12/49
10605	1/50
10627	2/50
10645	3/50
10670	4/50
10690	5/50
10716	6/50
10739	7/50
10762	8/50
10776	9/50
10806	10/50
10856	11/50
10865	12/50
10877	1/51
10904	2/51
10939	3/51
10940	4/51
10973	5/51
10991	6/51
11011	7/51
11024	8/51
11037	9/51
11072	10/51
11095	11/51
11114	12/51
11133	1/52

MGM	CON'T				
11165	2/52	12344	10/56	30384	7/51
11180	3/52	12369	11/56	30415	9/51
11206	4/52	12390	12/56	30494	1/52
11236	5/52	12408	1/57	30526	2/52
11253	6/52	12415	2/57	30582	6/52
11272	7/52	12449	3/57	30640	9/52
11292	8/52	12479	5/57	30669	11/52
11309	9/52	12490	6/57	30703	12/52
11347	10/52	12500	7/57	30724	1/53
11351	11/52	12529	8/57	30783	5/53
11386	12/52	11538	9/57	30802	9/53
11393	1/53	12558	10/57	30837	2/54
11425	2/53	12586	11/57	30845	4/54
11456	3/53	12599	12/57	30866	1/55
11490	5/53	12609	1/58	30881	7/55
11515	6/53	12616	2/58	30884	9/55
11545	7/53	12626	3/58	---------	
11561	8/53	12631	4/58	55001	2/55
11571	9/53	12655	5/58	55005	4/55
11587	10/53	12665	6/58	55009	6/55
11610	11/53	12688	7/58	55010	7/55
11645	12/53	12700	8/58	55012	10/55
11655	1/54	12706	9/58	55013	11/55
11680	2/54	12718	10/58	55014	3/56
11702	3/54	12731	11/58	---------	
11717	4/54	12741	12/58	(CUB)	
11736	5/54	12746	1/59	9001	4/58
11764	6/54	12760	2/59	9005	6/58
11767	7/54	12770	3/59	9012	7/58
11798	8/54	12784	4/59	9013	8/58
11802	9/54	12797	5/59	9015	9/58
11846	10/54	12808	6/59	9017	10/58
11857	11/54	12814	7/59	9018	11/58
11891	12/54	12817	8/59	9021	1/59
11908	1/55	12828	9/59	9024	2/59
11919	2/55	12833	10/59	9027	3/59
11948	3/55	12840	11/59	9029	4/59
11963	4/55	12853	12/59	9032	5/59
11991	5/55	---------		9033	6/59
12002	6/55	30006	3/47	9035	7/59
12020	7/55	30007	4/47	9040	8/59
12045	8/55	30012	6/47	9047	9/59
12054	9/55	30015	7/47	9050	10/59
12073	10/55	30025	9/47		
12119	11/55	30048	1/48	---------	
12164	12/55	30058	2/48	(METRO)	
12165	1/56	30073	4/48	20001	10/58
12175	2/56	30226	1/50	20005	11/58
12198	3/56	30228	4/50	20011	12/58
12213	4/56	30255	8/50	20014	2/59
12252	5/56	30256	9/50	20018	3/59
12275	6/56	30279	11/50	20022	4/59
12296	7/56	30288	12/50	20023	5/59
12310	8/56	30334	2/51	20026	6/59
12325	9/56	30351	4/51	20027	8/59
		30360	5/51	20029	10/59
				20030	12/59

MGM CON'T
(ORBIT)
9001   3/58
SEE CUB

MGT
778   11/52

MICHELLE
365   4/57
366   5/57

MICOR
1   4/49

MIDDLETONE
001   8/51
008   4/56
011   11/56

2001   6/55
2002   11/55

MIDWEST
109   11/49

MIGHTY
111   2/59

MILE
101   3/59

MILESTONE
2001   6/59
2002   10/59

MILLAN
1118   5/59

MILLER
3264   11/57

MILLION
SEE MONEY

MILLS
777   8/58

MILO
102   12/59

MILTONE
218   7/47
227   11/47
246   4/48

1301   7/48

5201   7/48
5259   4/49
5261   6/49

6005   4/49

(FOTO)
160   4/48

(METRO)
7465   5/48
7474   1/49

8004   10/49
8006   12/49

(ROY MILTON)
110   2/47

(SACRED)
79   7/47
120   7/48
284   10/49

(3 MINUTES)
500   1/48

MINIT
605   12/59

MINK
021   6/59
022   11/59
----
100   8/59

MINOR
105   2/57

110   8/58
112   6/59
113   7/59

MIRACLE
103   5/47
119   12/47
126   4/48
129   10/48
131   2/49
132   3/49
136   7/49
146   10/49
----
507   5/49
(MASTER)
101   5/48

MIRANDA
4-55-1   10/55

4-66   3/56
----
55   12/55

3093   1/56

MIRROR
307   12/59

MISTENE
101   10/55

MMC
005   4/59

MMI
1234   5/58
1236   8/58
1239   12/58

MODE
1   10/57

MODERN
MODERN MUSIC
MODERN RECORDS
101   4/45

MODERN CON'T		860	3/52	(CROWN)	
102	5/45	875	7/52	101	12/53
111	8/45	877	8/52	104	1/54
123	3/46	882	9/52	105	2/54
139	8/46	888	11/52	111	4/54
145	10/46	892	12/53	115	5/54
147	3/47	894	1/53	116	6/54
152	9/47	899	3/53	120	7/54
157	1/48	902	4/53	122	8/54
158	4/48	903	5/53	127	9/54
---------		907	7/53	131	1/55
(Prefix for		911	8/53	141	2/55
following:		914	9/53	142	3/55
MM-20-)		915	10/53	145	4/55
510	1/47	917	11/53	148	5/55
514	3/47	924	2/54	152	6/55
523	6/47	925	3/54	153	7/55
527	9/47	927	4/54	158	8/55
528	10/47	930	5/54	160	9/55
559	1/48	933	7/54	---------	
568	3/48	936	8/54	(FLAIR)	
578	4/48	938	9/54	1004	5/53
584	6/48	940	10/54	1010	6/53
608	7/48	943	11/54	1013	8/53
613	9/48	947	1/55	1015	9/53
624	10/48	950	2/55	1016	10/53
643	12/48	955	4/55	1019	11/53
649	2/49	958	5/55	1021	12/53
663	6/49	959	6/55	1030	3/54
681	7/49	961	7/55	1034	4/54
693	8/49	962	8/55	1039	5/54
700	10/49	970	10/55	1042	7/54
721	11/49	971	11/55	1046	8/54
725	12/49	975	12/55	1050	9/54
726	1/50	981	2/56	1053	10/54
728	2/50	984	3/56	1060	12/54
737	3/50	986	4/56	1063	2/55
741	4/50	988	5/56	1065	3/55
742	5/50	989	6/56	1068	5/55
757	8/50	995	7/56	1070	6/55
768	9/50	997	8/56	1072	7/55
774	10/50	998	9/56	1074	8/55
785	11/50	1005	11/56	1077	9/55
788	12/50	1007	12/56	1078	11/55
791	1/51	1013	2/57	---------	
794	2/51	1019	5/57	(KENT)	
806	3/51	1022	6/57	300	3/58
809	4/51	1023	8/57	303	5/58
814	5/51	1025	9/57	304	7/58
822	6/51	1026	12/57	311	8/58
831	9/51	---------		313	9/58
839	10/51	(BLUES &		315	10/58
842	11/51		RHYTHM)	317	2/59
844	12/51	7000	2/52	325	6/59
856	2/52			---------	
				5001	9/56

MODERN
  (METEOR)
2002   5/58

5000   1/53
5002   3/53
5003   5/53
5006   6/53
5013   10/53
5014   9/54
5017   1/55
5018   5/55
5021   9/55
5022   10/55
5028   2/56
5030   5/56
5031   6/56
5035   7/56
5036   8/56
5046   8/58

  (RPM)
303   9/50
310   12/50
318   3/51
319   4/51
323   6/51
333   9/51
340   12/51
343   3/52
356   5/51
362   8/52
365   9/52
369   11/52
374   12/52
377   1/53
380   3/53
383   5/53
386   6/53
387   7/53
391   9/53
392   10/53
395   11/53
396   1/54
403   2/54
404   3/54
410   5/54
412   7/54
413   8/54
416   10/54
419   12/54
422   2/55
427   5/55
431   7/55
436   8/55
437   10/55

441   11/55
448   12/55
452   1/56
457   3/56
458   4/56
464   6/56
467   7/56
469   8/56
470   9/56
475   11/56
481   12/56
490   3/57
491   4/57
498   9/57
500   10/57
501   11/57
502   12/57

  (MODERN)
501   1/55

1026   12/49

4000   9/51

5000   2/55
5001   3/55

MODERN SOUND
6901   4/58
6902   6/58
6903   7/58
6905   9/58

MOHAWK
101   10/56
105   6/57

MOHAWK
101   1/59
103   2/59
111   12/59
----
201   12/59

MOKA
1000   6/59

MONA
101   8/59

MONARCH
702   5/53
703   10/53

3004   5/53
3005   11/53
3006   4/54

MONDI
106   4/51
108   12/51

MONEY
209   1/55
212   3/55
215   3/56
220   9/56

  (CASH)
1001   3/55
1014   9/55
1015   11/55
1019   1/56
1021   2/56
1035   6/56
1037   7/56

  (MILLION)
2004   5/54
2009   3/55
2011   5/55
2014   7/55

MONODE
100   12/58

MONOGRAM
111   2/49
110   3/49
116   4/49
125   5/49
141   7/49
147   11/49
154   12/49
156   3/50
----
401   11/52

MONOQUE
102   3/59

MONTE CARLO
no #   9/55
002   2/56
003   1/57
004   2/57

MONTELL
1002   12/58

2001   6/59

3001   6/59

MONUMENT
M-1   4/51

MONUMENT
400   10/58
401   12/58
402   2/59
403   3/59
405   6/59
407   7/59
409   9/59
410   11/59

MOOD
1011   7/53
1014   10/53
1017   2/54

MOON
105   8/59
----
302   8/59

MOONGLOW
5004   3/57
5006   4/57

MOONLIGHT
102   12/49

MOPIC
4207   9/59

7707   9/59

MOROCCO
1002   8/58
1005   9/58

MORRISON
39   6/51

M.O.S.S.
MOSS
M-O-S-S
001   12/56
002   6/57

MOST
713   5/59
716   7/59

MOTIFF
001   9/56
003   11/56
005   2/57
015   8/59

MOTIFF
007   9/49

2001   5/49
2002   8/49

MOTOR CITY
1005   7/53

MOUNTAIN
299   6/59

MOVIE LAND
66   12/50
71   7/51
84   9/52

MOVIECRAFT
605   11/57

M.P.C.C.
4204   5/59

M-R-C
600   10/58

MR. CRUM
801   8/58

MRL
6132   10/54

MRT
777   8/52

MUN-RAB
102   5/59
104   6/59

MUSIC
395   7/46

MUSIC
1042   10/53

MUSICART
101   1/50
103   6/50

MUSICART
318   2/55

MUSIC ART
751   3/46

MUSIC CITY
750   12/54
762   1/55
790   8/55
792   2/56
807   5/57
814   11/57

1118   2/57

MUSICDISC
2002   12/59

MUSIC FOR
SOCIETY
1502   11/45

MUSIC MASTER
SEE GOTHAM

MUSICO
2003   2/55

MUSICRAFT
314   2/45
318   3/45
322   4/45
326   9/45
347   2/46
353   5/46
394   8/46
409   9/46
423   11/46
443   1/47
456   8/47
----
505   8/47
508   9/47
532   1/48
546   3/48
554   4/48
557   5/48
571   6/48
578   7/48

15008   12/42
15010   1/43
15011   2/43
15017   3/44
15018   4/44
15019   9/44
15020   10/44
15021   1/45
15029   4/45
15038   6/45
15040   9/45
15044   11/45
15049   12/45
15054   2/46
15087   8/46
15090   9/46
15094   11/46
15098   1/47

MUSIQUE
107   10/53

MUTUAL
1   1/49
----
201   7/50
204   2/51
207   3/51

MYSTERY
1002   11/53

MYSTIC
0528   4/58

NABOR
5817   11/58

NAR
524   12/56

NASHBORO
SEE EXCELLO

NASCO
SEE EXCELLO

NATIONAL
1001   9/46

4001   4/46
4003   6/46
4004   7/46
4009   10/46
4010   11/46
4011   1/47
4014   3/47
4015   5/47
4017   5/48
4018   1/49

5001   7/45
5008   9/45
5009   12/45
5011   3/46
5012   4/46
5017   6/46

5019   5/48

6001   11/45
6002   1/46

7001   8/44
7006   12/44
7007   2/45
7008   4/45
7009   11/45
7010   2/46
7012   9/46
7013   12/46
7018   12/47
7023   5/48

8001   6/45

9001   10/44
9003   12/44
9005   1/45
9010   2/45
9011   4/45
9012   5/45
9014   7/45
9015   9/45
9016   12/45
9017   1/46
9018   3/46
9019   6/46
9020   9/46
9021   11/46
9022   12/46
9024   1/47
9026   2/47
9027   3/47
9029   4/47
9034   5/47
9035   6/47
9036   9/47
9038   10/47
9040   1/48
9042   2/48
9043   3/48
9044   5/48
9045   6/48
9046   7/48
9051   8/48
9055   9/48
9058   11/48
9063   12/48
9064   1/49
9067   2/49
9068   3/49
9071   4/49
9078   5/49

NATIONAL CON'T
9080	6/49
9085	8/49
9089	9/49
9090	10/49
9092	11/49
9095	12/49
9096	1/50
9102	2/50
9104	3/50
9105	4/50
9114	6/50
9117	7/50
9119	8/50
9127	10/50
9128	11/50
9139	12/50
9142	1/51
9147	2/51
9149	4/51

NATIONAL HEMOPHILIA FOUNDATION
101   6/58

NATIONAL RECORDING COMPANY
102	7/57
104	9/57
113	11/57
114	12/57

NATIONWIDE
2537   10/53

NATURAL
SEE JUBILEE

NAU-VOO
802	12/58
803	2/59
806	6/59
807	8/59

NEIL
104   2/57

NEMO
1005   1/51

NEPTUNE
107   10/59

NEPTUNE
1002   6/50

NEW DISC
5156	2/55
10011	10/54
10015	11/54
10018	2/55
10019	3/55

NEW JAZZ
801	7/49
817	2/50
864	12/51
80001	7/49

NEW ORLEANS
2	8/49
JW-4	8/49

NEW ORLEANS BAND WAGON
5   4/52

NEWPORT
7003   9/58

NEW SONG
116   6/58

NEWTONE
101   9/51

NEW TONE
2012   5/54

NOCTURNE
1003	5/55
49669	11/53

NOEL
1001   7/54

NORFOLK
1303   10/49

NORGOLDE
103   9/59

NORGRAN
SEE CLEF

NORMAN
6163   12/56

NORTH AMERICAN
505   10/50

NORTH STAR
2001	4/54
2002	6/54
2008	2/55
2011	5/55
2014	9/55

NORTH WESTERN
2338	5/54
2411	12/56

NORVA
1000   9/57

NOR-VA-JAK
1321	10/58
1322	11/58

NOSTALGIC
1002   3/59

NOTARY	
1003	7/50

NOTE	
10008	11/57

20000	12/56

NOVA	
103	10/55
104	12/55
109	1/57
116	6/57
118	11/57

NOVART	
21	7/57

NOW	
1008	7/58
1010	9/58

NRC	
001	3/58
004	5/58
005	6/58
006	7/58
011	11/58
015	12/58
021	2/59
023	3/59
027	6/59
033	7/59
036	8/59
040	9/59
042	10/59
047	11/59
049	12/59

500	5/58
502	8/58

5001	8/58
5003	10/58
5004	1/59
5008	6/59

N TONE	
102	4/59

NU ATK	
112	9/59

NU-CLEAR	
1180	4/58

5944	7/59

7651	9/59

8089	9/59

NUCRAFT	
100	6/59

NUCRAFT	
100	11/51
102	9/52
112	5/53
113	7/53
116	8/53
130	6/54

1010	1/53
1022	4/55
1024	12/55

2020	2/55
2023	6/55
2026	7/55

NUGGET	
1000	5/59
1001	6/59

NU KAT	
109	5/59
115	9/59

OAK	
102	10/56
103	5/58

O'CONNER	
0-100-1	12/47

0104	9/47

ODE	
1601	4/53

1700	8/53
1710	12/53

6300	12/53

O GEE	
100	1/59
102	5/59

OHIO	
1001	8/57

O.J.	
1006	2/57
1007	10/57
1010	12/57

OKEH	
SEE COLUMBIA	

OKLAHOMA	
5001	2/58
5005	6/58
5015	1/59
5018	4/59

OLD TIMER	
7003	7/54

8031	1/51

OLD TOWN	
300	12/56
304	5/57
305	6/57

1014	9/55
1015	12/55
1017	2/56
1019	4/56
1022	6/56
1027	7/56
1029	11/56
1034	2/57
1038	3/57
1047	2/58

OLD TOWN
CON'T
1055   7/58
1056   9/58
1059   10/58
1061   12/58
1066   1/59
1068   5/59
1073   8/59
1074   10/59

OLIVER
15   8/47

OL' PODNER
101   2/59
102   4/59

OLYMPIC
501   8/55
502   10/55
503   11/55

OMEGA
109   3/52
110   6/54

OMEGA
101   2/58
118   12/58

ON-BEAT
101   6/59

1-O-A
100   10/52
103   4/53

1-O-1
100   2/56

ON THE SQUARE
315   3/59

ONYX
217   2/56

506   1/57
508   3/57
510   4/57
511   6/57

ONYX
2007   9/51

OPAL
0113   12/58
----
600   6/59

1212   6/59

OPAL
205   2/49
212   12/49

OPAL
579   6/53
----
653   8/53

OPERA
1014   1/51

OPPORTUNE
2   12/53

50263   12/53

ORANGE
1002   6/59

ORBIT
2   4/55
----
101   3/56
102   4/56
107   1/57
----
506   3/58
507   5/58
515   7/58
516   9/58
521   11/58
529   1/59

532   3/59
540   4/59
545   5/59

ORBIT
SEE MGM

ORBIT SOUND
113   1/58

ORCHID
1   12/49

ORFEO
SEE ALADDIN

ORGAN RHYTHMS
386   12/51
----
501   5/49

ORIGINAL
501   10/53
502   2/54
507   4/54
508   7/54
510   9/54
512   2/55
515   4/55
520   7/55
523   10/55
527   4/56
532   11/56
533   2/57

1014   11/52

1000   1/54
1006   1/55
1008   6/55

ORIGINAL SOUND
4   4/59
5   9/59
6   10/59

ORIOLE
101   8/50

ORIOLE	
319	4/59

1317	1/59
ORMOND	
101	12/55
ORO	
1	12/58

1318	3/59
1320	5/59

1501	9/59
OROCO	
5401	5/54

19531	5/53

195309	11/53
ORPHEUS	
255	1/48

1001	11/45
ORPHEUS	
1101	2/56
OSCAR	
102	3/52
107	7/54
OTIS	
735	3/50
OXFORD	
7374	10/55
OZARK	
102	10/56

PACE	
101	2/59
PACIFIC	
601	12/45
602	2/46
603	3/46
604	4/46
607	5/46
612	6/46
617	8/46
621	9/46
625	11/46
626	12/46
627	3/47
632	6/47
PACIFIC JAZZ	
601	10/52
603	3/53
604	4/53
615	12/53
616	9/54
617	10/54
629	11/55
PACIFICA	
1001	12/54
PAL	
1001	3/56
1003	1/59
PALACE	
102	6/52
138	12/54
145	2/56
PALDA	
101	5/47
102	6/47
108	1/48
114	5/48
118	11/48
124	2/50

1001	2/48
1002	5/48
1012	8/48
1016	11/48

(ESSEX)	
301	2/52
302	3/52
303	4/52
306	8/52
309	11/52
311	1/53
315	2/53
321	4/53
325	6/53
327	7/53
331	8/53
332	10/53
335	11/53
341	12/53
343	1/54
346	2/54
353	3/54
354	5/54
361	6/54
364	8/54
371	10/54
375	11/54
386	2/55
391	4/55
397	6/55
398	7/55
401	9/55
402	10/55
406	11/55
407	12/55
410	2/56

703	2/50

(FLASH)	
103	2/52

(HOLIDAY)	
108	9/51
110	12/51
111	2/52

(SOMERSET)	
725	4/58

6600	9/58

(TRANS-WORLD)	
711	4/56
718	7/56

(VICTORIA)	
101	9/51
102	11/51

PALDA CON'T
(WHEELING)
1001   10/49

PALETTE
501   2/59

5007   9/58
5015   3/59
5020   6/59
5032   9/59
5035   10/59
5037   11/59
5040   12/59

PALLADIUM
600   8/58
605   12/59

PALM
100   12/54

PAM
106   9/59
----
201   9/59

PAMASOUS
6022   7/55

PAN (AMERICAN)
1   8/45
7   9/45

PANAMA
106   6/59

PANDORA
1000   11/59

PANORAMA
1001   4/59
1002   5/59

PAP
908   7/52

PAR
235   9/57

1303   11/52

PARADISE
120   6/48

PARADISE
109   5/59

2007   6/55
2009   3/56

PARAGON
500   10/47

PARIS
501   2/57
503   4/57
505   5/57
506   7/57
507   9/57
508   10/57
511   1/58
514   4/58
517   6/58
520   8/58
521   9/58
523   10/58
524   12/58
529   1/59
531   3/59
533   5/59
535   6/59
536   7/59
537   8/59
538   10/59
539   11/59

PARKER
10-102   8/52
10-104   11/52
10-107   5/53
----
114   12/55
115   3/56

PARK LANE
102   12/58

PARKWAY
501   4/50

PARKWAY
SEE CAMEO

PARROT
PARROTT
775   7/53
788   11/53
808   1/55
813   7/55
817   10/55
819   11/55
823   6/56

PAT
101   9/59

PATHWAY
2127   10/58

PATIO
2   4/56
----
100   6/58

PAVILION
776   6/50
782   2/51

PAVIS
101   3/54

PAYSON
104   10/58

PEACEFUL
    VALLEY
401   7/56

PEACH
703   5/58
724   7/58
----
711   12/58

PEACH CON'T

713	6/59
716	7/59
720	9/59
725	10/59

0563	3/59

0628	3/59

PEACOCK

800	8/58
801	4/59

1500	12/49
1504	1/50
1514	2/50
1516	3/50
1537	7/50
1544	9/50
1561	11/50
1567	2/51
1568	3/51
1569	4/51
1570	5/51
1572	6/51
1574	7/51
1577	9/51
1581	10/51
1586	12/51
1593	2/52
1594	4/52
1595	5/52
1602	8/52
1610	9/52
1611	1/53
1612	3/53
1614	4/53
1616	5/53
1621	7/53
1622	10/53
1626	11/53
1627	12/53
1631	2/54
1632	4/54
1637	6/54
1639	8/54
1644	12/54
1650	3/55
1651	5/55
1654	8/55
1658	2/56
1661	3/56
1663	4/56
1664	7/56

1668	11/56
1671	1/57
1673	5/57
1678	6/57
1681	11/57
1682	3/58
1683	6/58
1686	10/58
1688	3/59
1689	4/59

1700	5/52
1703	8/52
1705	9/52
1706	12/52
1708	1/53
1709	3/53
1712	5/53
1714	7/53
1720	10/53
1723	2/54
1724	3/54
1726	4/54
1731	7/54
1733	10/54
1740	1/55
1741	5/55
1747	6/55
1751	10/55
1757	1/56
1761	4/56
1763	6/56
1764	12/56
1771	1/57
1773	5/57
1777	6/57
1780	11/57
1782	4/58
1783	5/58
1785	6/58
1787	7/58
1788	11/59
1790	1/59
1792	3/59
1794	4/59
1797	5/59
1800	10/59

(BACK BEAT)

500	8/57
503	12/57
504	2/58
505	3/58
508	4/58
510	5/58
513	6/58

519	8/58
522	11/58
525	2/59
526	4/59
527	7/59
528	9/59
529	11/59

(DUKE)

103	8/52
105	11/52
107	1/53
108	2/53
110	4/53
112	6/53
116	9/53
117	12/53
120	2/54
122	3/54
124	4/54
128	5/54
129	7/54
131	9/54
135	12/54
136	1/55
137	4/55
141	5/55
142	6/55
144	7/55
145	8/55
147	10/55
148	1/56
149	2/56
150	4/56
151	5/56
153	6/56
154	7/56
157	9/56
159	10/56
160	11/56
161	12/56
164	1/57
167	3/57
175	6/57
176	7/57
177	9/57
178	11/57
182	2/58
184	4/58
185	5/58
190	6/58
196	7/58
199	10/58

200	4/53
201	6/53

PEACOCK CON'T
(DUKE)
202   9/53
204   12/53
205   4/54
206   7/54
207   12/54
208   7/55
211   11/55
213   12/56
214   2/57
----
301   11/58
304   1/59
305   2/59
306   4/59
307   5/59
308   7/59
309   8/59
313   11/59
315   12/59

3004   9/56
3012   2/57
3020   6/57

4000   9/56

(PROGRESSIVE
JAZZ)
108   6/53
----
500   7/52

PEAK
104   4/57
105   3/59

1001   12/58
1008   6/59

5000   8/57

PEAK
800   2/49

PEARL
11   10/46
20   6/48
25   5/49
----
50   7/46
73   7/50

271   2/52
----
300   11/50
----
400   11/50
----
600   6/50
----
700   2/52
----
800   2/50

1000   5/49

9000   6/54

PEARL
101   7/59
----
709   11/57
713   4/58

PEEK-A-BOO
101   3/58
102   4/58

PEERLESS
2358   1/47

PELICAN
106   10/53

530303   8/53

PEN-ART
1782   11/55
1850   3/56
1910   11/56

21283   11/55
21304   6/56

PENGUIN
501   3/48
503   4/48
506   5/48
----
858   7/49
859   12/49

PENGUIN
0691   8/57

PENNANT
329   6/55
331   8/55

PENNSYLVANIA
145   9/52
149   1/54

PENNY
100   7/59

PEP
102   11/49

PEP
101   6/55
104   3/56
106   7/56
109   1/57
115   3/58
117   5/58

PEPPER
866   7/58
888   10/58
896   3/59
910   11/59

PERFECT
108   3/56
109   8/56

2002   8/52

PERFORMANCE
500   3/59

PERRI
111   1/50

PERSONALITY
1002   9/59
1004   11/59

PERSPECTIVE
5001   8/54

PET
801   4/58
806   8/58

PETER PAN
12   5/50

2238   2/50

PETITE
501   12/57

PHASE
867   6/59

PHEASANT
101   12/57

PHENIX
SEE GOTHAM

PHILLIPS
INTERNATIONAL
SEE SUN

PHILO
SEE ALLADIN

PHOENIX
007   12/49
021   4/50
030   12/58

PHONOGRAPH
1022   5/58
1024   10/58
1026   12/58
1027   3/59

PIC
001   3/54
006   8/54

10   11/54
22   12/54
23   1/55
24   3/55
26   10/55

9341   10/59

PICA
115   7/59

PICKUP
1002   2/46

PICNIC
602   8/57

PICTURE
561   7/51

PIK
701   8/59

PILGRIM
702   2/56
704   4/56
715   7/56
719   10/56
720   11/56
722   12/56

24969   7/56

PILLAR
1   5/59

PILOTONE
5203   3/47

PIMNIC
1000   5/51

PINCUS
              PLATTER
102   4/59
103   8/59

2866   4/58

PINK
701   5/59

PINK CLOUD
796   3/59

PINKY
101   10/58

PIONEER
401   6/48
----
612   4/49

PIONEER INT.
101   7/59

PIP
100   10/59

PIPER
              PLATTERS
501   6/59

PIV
1004   11/56
1009   4/57

PLA-MOR
500   6/49

PLANET
100   9/57

1004   6/59

PLANET X
9623   2/58

PLATTER
106   2/58

PLAY
1005   12/58

PLAYBACK
1111   7/59

1198   3/59

PLAY ME
3517   9/59
3518   11/59
3519   12/59

PLAYTIME
184   5/52

PLAZA
SEE ATLANTIC

PLAZA
362   7/56

5006   4/57

PLAZA
1100   10/50

PLEASANT
101   8/47
106   3/48
108   11/48

PLEASANT
        PHEASANT
4   7/59

1188   5/59

PLUS
102   3/56
104   10/56

PLYMOUTH
1050   6/49

POINT
8   1/57
10   3/57
11   4/57

POLO
155   6/51

POOR BOY
107   12/59

POP
2703   12/57

POPLAR
101   8/57
103   10/57
104   11/57
118   2/58
139   9/58

POPPY
1001   12/58

2003   6/59
2004   8/59
2005   9/59

POP SACRED
7001   5/55

PORT
SEE JUBILEE

PORTA
1001   5/58

PORTER
1002   12/57

5010   2/58
5011   3/58
5012   4/58
5013   5/58

POTTER
4265   4/53

POWER
113   4/59
----
601   11/58

PRELUDE
100   1/53

PREMIER
100   6/44

1179   6/49

2078   3/44

20166   8/44

28990   9/44
28991   10/44
28992   11/44
28994   12/44
28995   1/45
29013   12/45
29022   6/49

PREMIER
151   6/59
----
501   9/55
----
601   11/58

PREMIER
2669   9/51

PREMIUM
850   6/50
860   9/50
865   12/50
871   4/51
874   5/51

PRESIDENT
10   8/47

1001   5/47

PRESIDENT
1004   8/55
1008   3/56
1009   4/56
1015   3/57
1016   5/57
1017   2/58

PRESTIGE
101   7/57
102   12/57
121   11/58
131   4/59
135   6/59
142   8/59
145   10/59
155   11/59
----
357   10/52
----
704   4/50
715   6/50
717   8/50
719   10/50
726   12/50
735   3/51
746   10/51
752   12/51
794   1/53
873   11/53
880   5/54
890   8/54
893   10/54
899   12/54
----
901   10/51
908   12/51
916   7/55

1000   10/50

PREVUE
1111   10/54

PREXY
403   1/59

PRI
101   10/59

PRIDE
101   10/59

3000   10/56

PRIMA
712   7/59

PRIMROSE
985   7/48

PRINCE
101   6/55

1076   3/56

1202   3/56
1204   11/58
1206   4/59
1207   9/59

PRINCESS
1   1/54
----
100   6/56

1035   12/51

PRIZE
705   5/50

6900   12/53

PRO
007   12/57

PROCESS
52   6/49
----
508   6/47
511   7/47
517   11/48
519   6/49
523   1/50

PROFILE
4002   10/58
4004   2/59

4005   4/59
4006   5/59

PROGRESSIVE
SEE PEACOCK

PROM
1009   3/52
1027   12/52
1058   11/53

PROTON
106   12/58
107   3/59
108   4/59
111   7/59
113   10/59
----
204   10/58

PRUDENTIA
101   6/49
105   8/49

PUBLIC
702   3/48
710   8/48

PURPLETONE
711   2/56

PURVIS
996   8/49

PYRAMID
100   11/50
----
199   3/51
----
251   5/51
----
300   5/53
----
371   5/53
----
401   9/51
----
900   6/52

PYRAMID
CON'T
902	8/52
903	9/52
913	7/54

2222	3/56
2225	1/59

3000	12/52
3011	1/54

3175	4/50

4000	10/54
4012	3/57
4014	5/57

Q
1008	11/55

Q-T
1047	4/57

QUAKER
103	11/47

QUALITY
715	8/54

1053	12/53

QUEEN
147	6/55
151	11/55

QUEEN
SEE KING

QUEST
101	7/56

QUICK
100	5/59

QUIP
101	6/58

RAB
901	2/51

RADAR
777	7/59

RADAX
70	11/53

145	11/53

RADIANT
64	5/54
75	6/54

106	8/57

120	11/51

1013	1/51

RADIO
101	3/58
103	4/58
105	5/58
107	6/58
108	7/58
112	8/58
114	9/58
119	2/59
123	4/59

RADIO ARTISTS
201	5/47
207	7/47
211	9/47
213	12/47
215	1/48
218	2/48
221	3/48
223	5/48
230	9/48
243	2/49
246	6/49
248	10/49
254	3/50
255	5/50
256	7/50
257	11/50

RAE COX
102	8/59

RAINBOW
105	4/51
141	10/51
147	12/51
157	1/52
165	4/52
177	6/52
179	9/52
201	1/53
214	5/53
219	7/53
226	11/53
235	1/54
240	2/54
243	4/54
252	5/54
260	8/54
261	9/54
264	10/54
270	11/54
280	3/55
292	6/55
316	7/55
332	4/56
344	6/56
355	8/56
377	12/56

301	6/52

1001	3/47

1001	5/51

4444	12/50

5002	11/47

6666	12/50

7777	2/51

8007	8/49

8888	2/51

7055	1/49

1204	12/57

8470	7/56

RAINBOW
CON'T
10007	4/47
10025	10/47
10031	11/47
10044	12/47
10060	4/48
10063	5/48
10083	7/48
10088	9/48
10091	1/49

11122	12/50

30033	10/50

30101	3/47

30201	3/47

30301	3/47

30401	4/47

30501	10/47

30601	5/47

30901	4/47

31001	8/47

40088	6/50

50001	3/47
50004	10/47

50088	5/50

60001	3/48
60005	4/48

60070	3/50

70013	7/48

70055	12/48

80077	8/49

90088	2/50

RAINBOW
        PLATTEN
311	4/55

RAKRIK
100	3/59

RAM
1106	7/59

8771	7/57

12127	8/59

R.A.M.
1549	7/59

RAMA
SEE TICO

RAMBLER
554	6/59

RANCH
1001	11/51

RANCH, J. R.
12	1/54

1428	9/52

RANCH HOUSE
10419	2/53

RANCHO
703	1/47

R & B
1301	9/54
1303	10/54
1304	11/54
1306	12/54
1310	1/55

R & B
6901	3/58

R & F
1326	9/59

1329	12/59

R & H
001	5/58

R & M
617	11/58

RANGELAND
1914	3/55

RANSON
100	11/58

RAVE
1001	5/57

2001	6/59

RAVEN
413	9/47
414	11/47
415	1/48

RAVEN
001	5/59

RAY
300	11/58
301	3/59

1382	8/59

RAYMOR
5003	10/48
5008	3/50

6001	3/54

RAYNOTE
2	6/59
4	8/59

RAZORBACK
101	4/58

RAZORBACK
CON'T

102	7/58
104	8/58
105	3/59

RCA VICTOR

26412	1/40
26481	2/40
26535	3/40
26542	4/40
26579	5/40
26607	6/40
26644	7/40
26665	8/40
26730	9/40
26750	10/40
26784	11/40
27219	12/40
27254	1/41
27287	2/41
27338	3/41
27360	4/41
27391	5/41
27435	6/41
27483	7/41
27527	8/41
27586	9/41
27598	10/41
27666	11/41
27703	12/41
27725	1/42
27777	2/42
27801	3/42
27837	4/42
27870	5/42
27891	6/42
27923	7/42
27940	8/42
27953	9/42
27972	10/42

PREFIX 20-

1504	10/42
1521	1/43
1524	2/43
1527	3/43
1530	6/43
1535	7/43
1539	9/43
1546	12/43
1547	1/44
1556	2/44
1563	3/44

1574	4/44
1584	5/44
1587	7/44
1591	8/44
1595	9/44
1596	10/44
1600	11/44
1608	12/44
1629	1/45
1636	2/45
1642	3/45
1656	4/45
1665	5/45
1672	6/45
1696	7/45
1711	8/45
1721	9/45
1727	10/45
1737	11/45
1763	12/45
1791	1/46
1793	2/46
1812	3/46
1842	4/46
1866	5/46
1870	6/46
1924	7/46
1960	9/46
1979	10/46
1999	11/46
2037	12/46
2090	1/47
2106	2/47
2143	3/47
2209	4/47
2251	5/47
2315	6/47
2344	7/47
2364	8/47
2468	9/47
2497	10/47
2559	11/47
2582	12/47
2651	1/48
2686	2/48
2757	3/48
2838	4/48
2902	5/48
2919	6/48
3013	7/48
3085	8/48
3108	9/48
3153	10/48
3176	11/48
3259	12/48
3309	1/49

3358	2/49
3381	3/49
3443	4/49
3451	5/49
3460	6/49
3482	7/49
3526	8/49
3531	9/49
3544	10/49
3575	11/49
3597	12/49
3623	1/50
3681	2/50

PREFIX 20/47-

3686	3/50
3752	4/50
3771	5/50
3819	6/50
3839	7/50
3878	8/50
3905	9/50
3933	10/50
3953	11/50
3980	12/50
4015	1/51
4054	2/51
4074	3/51
4112	4/51
4133	5/51
4158	6/51
4190	7/51
4212	8/51
4247	9/51
4297	10/51
4363	11/51
4401	12/51
4446	1/52
4504	2/52
4554	3/52
4632	4/52
4681	5/52
4750	6/52
4825	7/52
4862	8/52
4927	9/52
4959	10/52
5023	11/52
5080	12/52
5116	1/53
5155	2/53
5213	3/53
5251	4/53
5289	5/53
5322	6/53
5363	7/53

RCA-VICTOR
CON'T

PREFIX 20/47-

5393	8/53
5432	9/53
5460	10/53
5505	11/53
5580	1/54
5644	2/54
5675	3/54
5707	4/54
5729	5/54
5764	6/54
5786	7/54
5830	8/54
5841	9/54
5871	10/54
5919	11/54
5955	12/54
5975	1/55
6027	2/55
6059	3/55
6072	4/55
6126	5/55
6146	6/55
6175	7/55
6227	8/55
6237	9/55
6272	10/55
6331	11/55
6357	12/55
6389	1/56
6420	2/56
6476	3/56
6499	4/56
6518	5/56
6541	6/56
6588	7/56
6619	8/56
6636	9/56
6682	10/56
6713	11/56
6749	12/56
6800	1/57
6815	2/57
6830	3/57
6880	4/57
6904	5/57
6938	6/57
6952	7/57
7005	8/57
7019	9/57
7056	10/57
7081	11/57
7112	12/57

7135	1/58
7160	2/58
7181	3/58
7209	4/58
7234	5/58
7265	6/58
7292	7/58
7312	8/58
7330	9/58
7353	10/58
7397	11/58
7426	12/58

PREFIX 47-

7439	1/59
7462	2/59
7474	3/59
7505	4/59
7525	5/59
7542	6/59
7557	7/59
7571	8/59
7593	9/59
7607	10/59
7637	11/59
7649	12/59

PREFIX 10-

1025	10/42
1329	11/47

PREFIX 21-

0000	1/49
0005	2/49
0031	3/49
0038	4/49
0060	5/49
0065	6/49
0086	7/49
0092	8/49
0111	10/49
0141	11/49
0155	1/50
0168	2/50

PREFIX 21/48-

0208	3/50
0310	4/50
0328	5/50
0348	6/50
0355	7/50
0367	8/50
0378	9/50
0390	10/50
0401	11/50

0408	12/50
0430	2/51
0439	3/51
0455	4/51
0466	5/51
0476	6/51
0489	7/51
0498	8/51

PREFIX 22-

0001	1/49
0004	2/49
0010	3/49
0016	4/49
0022	6/49
0037	7/49
0039	8/49
0044	9/49
0046	10/49
0049	11/49
0060	12/49
0061	2/50

PREFIX 22/50-

0070	4/50
0083	5/50
0088	6/50
0092	7/50
0095	8/50
0100	9/50
0103	10/50
0105	11/50
0106	12/50
0109	1/51
0112	2/51
0117	3/51
0119	4/51
0126	5/51
0130	6/51
0136	7/51
0140	8/51

PREFIX 23-

0288	8/46
1470	1/50
1481	2/50
1550	3/50
1574	4/50

PREFIX 25-

0057	2/46
1146	1/50

PREFIX 25/51-

RCA VICTOR
CON'T

PREFIX 25/51-

1150	3/50
1156	4/50
1164	6/50
1166	7/50
1168	8/50
1172	9/50
1176	10/50
1179	11/50
1181	12/50
1185	1/51
1187	2/51
1189	3/51
1194	4/51
1196	5/51
1198	6/51
1202	7/51
1204	8/51

PREFIX 28-

0405	2/46

PREFIX 40-

4003	1/47

PREFIX 46-

0011	11/47

----

45 RPM SERIES
4/49 to 3/50

PREFIX 47-

2718	4/49
2929	6/49

PREFIX 48-

0142	11/49
0152	12/49
0170	1/50
0179	2/50

PREFIX 50-

0016	6/49
0019	7/49
0038	11/49
0040	12/49
0046	1/50

0050	2/50
0054	3/50

(BLUEBIRD)

8443	6/40
8463	7/40
8484	8/40
8509	9/40
8535	10/40
8602	1/41
8614	2/41
8631	3/41
8656	4/41
8870	12/41
8884	1/42
8934	3/42
8958	4/42
8983	5/42
9010	6/42
9011	7/42
9024	8/42
9035	9/42
9040	10/42

10506	1/40
10591	2/40
10616	3/40
10652	4/40
10685	5/40
10726	6/40
10767	7/40
10800	8/40
10840	9/40
10872	10/40
10904	11/40
10944	12/40
10982	1/41
11016	2/41
11050	3/41
11091	4/41
11123	5/41
11164	6/41
11199	7/41
11231	8/41
11281	9/41
11304	10/41
11332	11/41
11367	12/41
11401	1/42
11442	2/42
11472	3/42
11493	4/42
11522	5/42
11538	6/42
11552	7/42

11562	8/42
11577	9/42
11586	10/42

PREFIX 30-

0010	10/49
0019	12/49

PREFIX 30-

0801	10/42
0802	11/42
0803	1/43
0809	2/43
0811	3/43
0812	4/43
0813	7/43
0816	8/43
0818	9/43
0819	1/44
0822	3/44
0823	4/44
0825	6/44
0826	7/44
0827	8/44
0830	11/44
0831	12/44
0834	1/45
0837	2/45

PREFIX 31-

0001	7/49
0010	8/49

PREFIX 32-

0004	8/49

PREFIX 33-

0500	11/42
0501	12/42
0502	2/43
0503	3/43
0504	6/43
0505	7/43
0506	8/43
0507	9/43
0509	3/44
0510	4/44
0513	6/44
0514	7/44
0515	9/44
0518	1/45
0523	3/45

RCA VICTOR
CON'T
BLUEBIRD
PREFIX 33-

0524	4/45
0527	5/45
0529	6/45
0531	8/45
0535	9/45
0537	11/45
0539	12/45

PREFIX 34-

0700	10/42
0701	11/42
0702	12/42
0704	1/43
0705	3/43
0707	7/43
0709	2/44
0710	4/44
0714	6/44
0715	7/44
0716	8/44
0718	11/44
0719	12/44
0722	2/45
0723	3/45
0727	4/45
0741	1/46
0746	3/46
0748	4/46

PREFIX 35-

0001	7/49

(GROOVE)

0001	2/54
0004	3/54
0010	4/54
0013	5/54
0020	6/54
0025	7/54
0032	8/54
0036	9/54
0038	11/54

0100	3/55
0104	4/55
0106	5/55
0108	6/55
0115	7/55
0116	8/55

0121	10/55
0127	11/55
0129	12/55
0136	1/56
0139	2/56
0141	3/56
0149	4/56
0153	5/56
0157	6/56
0159	7/56
0161	8/56
0165	9/56
0169	10/56
0173	11/56
0177	12/56

("X")

0001	2/54
0004	3/54
0011	4/54
0012	5/54
0021	6/54
0033	7/54
0040	8/54
0051	9/54
0056	10/56
0070	11/56
0075	12/56
0081	1/55
0097	2/55
0105	3/55
0110	4/55
0129	5/55
0138	6/55
0146	7/55
0154	8/55
0161	9/55
0166	10/55
0174	11/55
0184	12/54

(VIK)

0189	1/56
0192	2/56
0196	3/56
0202	4/56
0210	5/56
0213	6/56
0218	7/56
0222	8/56
0226	9/56
0232	10/56
0242	11/56
0244	12/56
0250	1/57
0259	2/57
0260	3/57

0269	4/57
0274	5/57
0278	6/57
0281	7/57
0286	8/57
0291	9/57
0304	11/57
0309	12/57
0315	1/58
0317	2/58
0322	3/58
0323	4/58
0327	5/58
0331	6/58
0332	7/58
0335	8/58
0337	9/58

R-DELL

11	12/56

101	4/58
103	5/58
105	6/58

602	6/58

RE-GO

100	8/46

1001	6/46
1002	1/47
1016	2/48

REAL

1301	7/55
1303	11/55
1304	1/56
1307	3/56
1308	4/56
1311	6/56
1313	8/56
1314	9/56

REBEL

1313	10/58

RECORDED IN
          HOLLYWOOD
SEE HOLLYWOOD

RECORDS
2001   11/51

RECORTE
401   2/58
402   5/58
404   10/58
412   6/59
415   10/59

RED BARN
1174   6/48

RED BIRD
1007   10/48
1008   8/50
1011   1/51
1021   11/55

1181   4/48
1200   8/57

10001   10/48

RED ROBIN
SEE FURY

REDD-E
002   3/54

1002   5/54
1011   7/58
1015   8/58

5003   11/58
5006   4/59
5007   5/59

REDHEAD
100   3/59

RED JAY
100   9/48

1006   7/50

RED SKIN
1001   12/48

RED TOP
105   6/58

REED
605   2/59

1016   11/58
1020   1/59
1023   8/59
1029   10/59

REEL
1013   3/59

REELFOOT
1249   5/58

REGAL
SEE KING
SEE DELUXE

REGAL
205   10/49

1196   9/49
1198   10/49
1205   11/50
1207   12/50

3231   9/49
3236   10/49
3241   12/49
3245   1/50
3260   2/50
3262   5/50
3270   6/50
3298   10/50
3300   11/50
3302   12/50
3306   1/51
3312   2/51
3313   3/51
3321   4/51
3324   6/51
3327   8/51

5067   11/49
5069   2/50

(R.F.D.)
5075   3/51

5077   5/51
5078   6/51
5082   8/51

REGAL
101   9/56

7501   4/58
7503   7/58
7505   9/58

REGENCY
664   9/57

REGENT
SEE SAVOY

REGIS
106   11/43

1008   9/44
1015   1/46

6000   5/46

7000   12/45

(MANOR)
100   2/46
102   1/47

1000   1/45
1002   3/45
1004   4/45
1005   5/45
1014   11/45
1016   2/46
1018   3/46
1020   5/46
1032   8/46
1040   9/46
1041   10/46
1042   12/46
1048   1/47
1056   2/47
1060   3/47
1067   5/47
1071   7/47
1078   8/47
1091   9/47
1094   10/47
1099   12/47

REGIS CON'T
MANOR
1106   1/48
1112   2/48
1126   4/48
1141   10/48
1145   11/48
1166   2/49
1171   3/49
1175   4/49
1177   5/49
1182   6/49
1187   7/49
1195   8/49

(ARCO)
1201   11/49
1221   12/49
1222   1/50
1234   3/50
1259   8/50

RE-GO
100   8/46
105   2/47

1001   6/46
1002   1/47
1004   2/47
1006   6/47
1011   9/47
1015   1/48
1016   2/48

REGO
1003   7/56

REINA
101   4/48
103   12/48

REINA
807   5/55

REJECT
1001   4/56

RELAX
L1   2/50
----

13   2/50

RELIGIOUS
    RECORDINGS
No #   5/49

RELIGIOUS
        TONE
700   11/49

REMINGTON
16001 9/51

25001 9/51
25024 3/52
25025 4/52

REMO
1022   6/59

REMSEN
102   2/57
103   8/57
105   10/58

RENDEZVOUS
100   3/58
101   4/58
102   11/58
103   2/59
104   3/59
105   5/59
108   6/59
109   7/59
111   8/59
112   11/59

RENDEZVOUS
812   10/54

RENOWN
101   9/57
104   1/58
108   6/59
109   7/59
110   9/59
112   10/59

RENOWN
5001   6/52

REPLICA
100   3/58
----
101   3/54
106   6/54

2000   8/53

5002   3/54

REPUBLIC
005   6/48
----
110   10/47
115   7/48
----
150   7/48

REPUBLIC
100   1/53

2001   11/59

7000   8/52
7013   9/52
7015   11/52
7017   12/52
7019   1/53
7023   2/53
7027   3/53
7043   5/53
7051   7/53
7053   9/53
7057   10/53
7059   11/53
7066   12/53
7067   2/54
7077   4/54
7084   5/54
7086   8/54
7103   12/54
7104   1/55
7107   3/55
7112   4/55
7119   10/55
7120   12/55
7123   1/56
7126   3/56

(JAMBOREE)

REPUBLIC
CON'T
(JAMBOREE)
501	7/50
510	8/50
513	9/50
514	11/50

(TENNESSEE)	
113	5/51
118	6/52
128	8/52

711	1/50
712	4/50
714	5/50
717	7/50
720	8/50
721	9/50
728	11/50
745	3/51
755	4/51
765	5/51
775	6/51
783	7/51
800	11/51
809	4/52
826	5/52
834	8/52
841	11/52

REQUEST
733	11/56

2004	9/56
2005	3/59
2008	11/59

3003	7/57
3006	6/58
3007	7/58

RESERVE
101	11/55
103	2/56
105	4/56
108	6/56
109	7/56
112	11/56
115	2/57
116	3/57
118	4/57

REV
3501	6/57

REVEAL
999	4/53

REX
777	11/55

REX
1008	8/59

REX
23005	5/49

REXFORD
104	6/51

RFD
SEE REGAL

RHAPSODY
101	5/46
122	5/47

2673	10/49

RHUMBOOGIE
4001	11/45

RHYMAIRES
1	6/59

RHYTHM
SEE TRILON

RHYTHM
104	5/57
126	8/59

1001	1/52
1003	5/52
1039	10/58

2009	4/56

RHYTHM AND
BLUES
100	3/53

RIALTO
401	7/53

600	11/52

RIALTO
1005	8/49

RIBBON
6903	10/59
6907	11/59

RIC
957	9/58
960	2/59
961	3/59
962	8/59
964	12/59

RICH
250	6/48

RICH
408	4/55

RICHLOG
101	10/56
102	11/56

RICHMOND
001	11/59

RICHMOND
148	3/50

1347	4/49

RICH-R'-TONE
304	11/51

402	5/47
405	7/47

RICH-R'-TONE
CON'T
415	12/47
446	4/49
451	7/49
453	9/49
454	11/49
460	1/50
475	4/50

619	8/52

701	4/50
702	5/50

802	7/51

1002	2/51
1023	9/51
1041	7/52
1045	8/52
1057	5/54

RICHTONE
312	12/51
314	1/53
352	4/53

RIDGE CLIMBER
1401	6/59

RIDGECREST
1001	2/59
1003	3/59

1101	2/59
1103	5/59
1105	6/59

1201	2/59
1202	3/59
1204	6/59

RIDGEWAY
011	8/59

111	10/55
113	3/56

713	7/59

RIETY
1016	10/59

RIGG
64000	11/59

RIGHTMAN
1020	7/49

RIH
SEE HOLLYWOOD

RIK
572	11/59

RIM
2016	3/56
2017	7/57
2021	5/58
2022	1/59

RING
10	3/58

100	12/55

500	10/57

RIP
126	4/58
135	7/58
138	9/58

190	6/58
202	10/58

12558	3/58

RITA
101	11/52
104	5/53
105	8/53
107	1/54
110	8/54
113	4/55
116	5/55

RITA
1003	12/59

RIVERMONT
102	3/58

1158	3/58

RIVERSIDE
425	9/59

612	6/58

RIVIERA
112	7/50

988	3/55

5171	11/54

RKO-UNIQUE
SEE UNIQUE

RMP
1005	1/55
1008	6/59

ROANI
1701	4/49

ROB
491	10/49

ROBBINS
1001	9/57
1002	1/58
1003	3/58
1005	6/58
1006	7/58
1009	8/58

ROBIN
SEE FURY

ROBIN
491	10/49

ROBIN CON'T
1001   10/48

ROBIN
1000   1/51
1001   4/51

ROBIN
1001   12/57
1003   2/58
1006   3/58
1007   4/58

ROC
901   2/58

5101   4/59

ROCKET
1   3/51

ROCKET
5493   4/58

122357   4/58

ROCKIN'
SEE KING

ROCKIN'
1   9/59

ROCK 'N' ROLL
609   7/55

RODEO
116   4/56
119   12/56
121   3/57
122   6/57
126   10/57
128   1/58
----
211   4/59

ROFILE
4001   7/58

ROLAND
1700   3/50
1701   5/50

ROLIN
5050   7/50

ROLLS
101   3/56

ROMAN
300   11/57

ROMAN III
400   2/58

RON
320   3/59
324   7/59
326   10/59
328   12/59

RONDO
128   4/48
129   5/48
146   7/48
150   10/48
154   11/48
157   12/48
187   3/49
188   4/49
192   7/49
199   10/49
214   1/50
221   2/50
222   3/50
225   4/50
238   7/50
239   8/50
261   5/51
300   7/52
301   2/53
303   4/53
----
623   11/50
625   2/51

907   8/55

1501   5/58

1554   2/49

5005   4/50

RONDON
1099   12/57

RONEL
107   11/55
109   3/56
111   10/56

RONENU
717   4/55

RON-MAR
1004   4/59

RONNEX
1001   4/55
1004   2/56

1184   1/57

ROO
106   6/59

ROOST
SEE ROYAL
        ROOST

RORK
003   3/53
----
78   7/52

ROSCO
409   7/59
411   10/59

ROSE
101   3/55
102   11/55
112   6/58

ROSE BETH
7419   10/58
- - - - - - - - - -
78500   8/58

ROSEMARY
1001   10/52
1002   12/52

ROULETTE
7000   9/55

ROULETTE
4001   2/57
4003   3/57
4010   4/57
4012   5/57
4013   6/57
4017   7/57
4020   9/57
4027   10/57
4032   11/57
4037   12/57
4043   1/58
4046   2/58
4056   3/58
4066   4/58
4073   5/58
4079   6/58
4085   7/58
4093   8/58
4102   9/58
4110   10/58
4116   11/58
4122   12/58
4126   1/59
4128   2/59
4139   3/59
4147   4/59
4154   5/59
4160   6/59
4170   7/59
4173   8/59
4184   9/59
4197   10/59
4201   11/59
4215   12/59
- - - - - - - - - -
7001   9/57
7003   11/57
7005   1/58
- - - - - - - - - -

(CASINO)
102   7/58
103   9/58
104   2/59
- - - - - - - - - -
(GONE)
5005   6/57
5014   12/57
5021   2/58
5023   3/58
5027   4/58
5028   5/58
5033   6/58
5037   7/58
5039   9/58
5044   10/58
5045   12/58
5051   2/59
5058   4/59
5059   5/59
5065   6/59
5066   7/59
5079   10/59
5083   11/59
- - - - - - - - - -
(MARK-X)
7006   12/57
7008   1/58
- - - - - - - - - -
8000   12/59

ROUND
101   4/53
103   12/53

ROUND
1009   6/59

ROUND UP
502   4/56

ROX
451   3/59

ROY MILTON
SEE MILTONE

ROY RECORDS
1002   6/45

2012   6/45

ROYAL
100   9/55

ROYAL
1004   5/59

ROYAL AUDIO
MUSIC
548   5/59
- - - - - - - - - -
1478   8/58

ROYALE
156   7/51
- - - - - - - - - -
330   7/51
338   9/51
341   10/51
- - - - - - - - - -
8094   7/51
8097   9/51
8100   10/51

ROYAL ROOST
509   3/50
512   8/50
518   11/50
520   12/50
523   2/51
526   5/51
530   10/51
536   12/51
543   2/52
573   9/53
581   11/53
585   4/54
592   8/54
597   10/54
598   1/55
608   7/55
610   10/55
612   11/55
614   12/55
617   3/56
621   10/56
624   12/56
628   4/57
- - - - - - - - - -
603   5/50

ROYAL ROOST
CON'T
607	6/50
608	8/50
612	10/50
613	12/50
614	1/51
615	2/51
616	6/51
617	8/51

1023	3/50

1242	12/50

(SCOOTER)
301	12/52
305	6/53

ROYAL-TONE
1001	8/48
1002	10/48

ROYALTY
SEE SAVOY

ROYALTY
213	7/55

ROYCE
0001	8/59

RPM
SEE MODERN

RRC
103	9/56
104	10/56

RUBY
100	10/55

101	2/54

100	2/57
110	2/57
120	2/57
130	2/57
150	2/57

200	2/57
220	2/57
280	7/57
290	2/57

320	5/57
390	5/57
410	5/57
430	5/57
470	7/57

550	6/58

724	7/57

1000	7/56

RUDDER
207	1/53

1001	3/52
1006	2/53

RURAL RHYTHM
502	10/55
503	12/55
504	7/56
506	12/56
507	2/57
510	6/57
514	4/59
518	6/59
521	7/59

RUSTIC
1926	2/57

SABRE
SEE CHANCE

SABRINA
101	4/59

SACRED
SEE MILTONE

SACRED
455	11/53
465	6/54

SAFARI
1004	11/57

SAGA
1000	12/57

SAGE
110	11/57

251	11/57
252	12/57
269	7/58
270	9/58
274	10/58
276	12/58
279	1/59
282	2/59
291	4/59
293	5/59
297	6/59
298	7/59
299	8/59
304	10/59

SAGE
1002	3/53

SAGE AND SOUND
180	10/54
205	6/55

SAKS
5012	5/48

SALEM
184	5/57

1001	4/57
1002	5/57
1005	6/57
1006	7/57
1010	8/57
1012	9/57
1014	10/57

2150	7/57

SALVATION
102   11/49

SAMSON
130   11/58
----
888   6/55

SAN
207   4/59

SAN ANTONIO
101   4/46

SANDEE
310   3/55

S & G
11   7/47

3003   7/47
3004   8/47

5000   5/54
5004   6/54
5008   11/54
5009   1/55

S & S
2025   11/58

SAND
145   7/57
----
258   12/57

SANDY
1001   9/57
1005   12/57
1007   2/58
1009   3/58
1010   4/58
1012   7/58
1013   8/58
1014   9/58
1017   3/59
1022   8/59
1024   9/59

SANDYLAND
1001   6/59

SANTA
6959   9/52

SANTEFE
100   6/59

SAN-TONE
126   7/59

SAPPHIRE
100   10/55
----
151   8/56

SAPPHIRE
705   2/47
709   3/47
712   9/47

SAR
101   11/59

SARG
103   5/54
104   8/54
110   10/54
117   7/55
118   8/55
123   12/55
128   4/56
132   6/56
140   9/56
147   12/56
148   1/57
156   5/57
158   4/58
160   7/58
164   3/59
165   8/59

SATURN
?   9/50

SAVOY
100   12/42
101   1/43
107   4/43
110   9/43
117   11/43
119   1/44
124   2/44
130   3/44
140   4/44
----
300   11/44
----
330   9/54
----
501   4/44
504   6/44
512   7/44
519   8/44
520   11/44
525   12/44
537   3/45
546   4/45
569   9/45
570   12/45
590   1/46
601   3/46
602   5/46
604   7/46
615   8/46
629   10/46
644   1/47
647   4/47
652   7/47
654   9/47
656   10/47
660   12/47
662   2/48
663   4/48
666   6/48
670   8/48
672   9/48
677   10/48
679   12/48
682   1/49
688   4/49
698   6/49
704   8/49
718   11/49
731   1/50
732   2/50
734   3/50
736   4/50
741   5/50
751   6/50
752   7/50

SAVOY CON'T					
756	8/50	1157	4/55	4021	11/50
761	9/50	1162	6/55	4025	5/51
762	10/50	1163	7/55	4026	7/51
766	11/50	1168	8/55	4027	8/51
773	12/50	1169	9/55	4028	10/51
775	1/51	1174	11/55	4029	12/51
777	2/51	1176	12/55	4031	2/52
778	3/51	1184	2/56	4034	5/52
784	5/51	1187	3/56	4037	7/52
791	6/51	1188	4/56	4039	9/52
801	8/51	1189	5/56	4040	11/52
816	9/51	1196	6/56	4044	4/53
821	11/51	1197	9/56	4045	8/53
827	12/51	----------		4047	11/53
830	1/52	1500	9/56	4049	1/54
835	2/52	1502	10/56	4051	5/54
842	4/52	1505	11/56	4055	7/54
844	5/52	1508	12/56	4060	1/55
847	6/52	1509	3/57	4063	3/55
852	7/52	1512	4/57	4066	5/55
856	8/52	1513	5/57	4071	2/56
859	9/52	1514	6/57	4073	3/56
864	10/52	1517	8/57	4075	4/56
868	11/52	1521	9/57	4076	10/56
872	12/52	1522	10/57	4077	12/56
878	1/53	1526	11/57	4081	3/57
884	2/53	1527	12/57	4088	12/57
887	3/53	1529	1/58	4090	2/58
889	4/53	1530	2/58	4092	3/58
893	5/53	1532	3/58	4097	7/58
898	6/53	1534	5/58	4101	8/58
----------		1539	6/58	4116	4/59
904	1/47	1544	7/58	4118	6/59
905	5/47	1549	8/58	----------	
909	11/47	1555	9/58	4500	7/57
932	9/48	1556	12/58	----------	
936	10/48	1558	2/59	5510	8/44
----------		1561	3/59	5511	11/44
1005	12/45	1564	4/59	5517	12/44
1075	5/46	1567	5/59	5526	4/46
----------		1568	6/59	5531	8/46
1100	7/53	1572	7/59	5533	1/47
1103	9/53	1576	9/59	5536	6/47
1107	10/53	1579	11/59	5541	11/47
1115	11/53	----------		5545	2/48
1118	12/53	2002	8/54	5548	4/48
1124	4/54	----------		5550	5/48
1128	5/54	2010	9/48	5551	7/48
1131	7/54	----------		5556	12/48
1133	8/54	3012	4/47	5557	1/49
1134	9/54	3023	12/49	5560	3/49
1138	10/54	----------		5561	4/49
1145	1/55	4002	2/49	----------	
1153	2/55	4013	10/49	6000	7/49
1154	3/55	4018	8/50	6046	12/57
		4019	10/50	----------	

SAVOY CON'T
8000	5/46
8005	1/48
8501	5/52

(ACORN)
305	10/50
316	3/51
319	5/51
323	7/51

(DEE GEE)
3065	4/53
3401	2/53
3402	4/53
3501	4/53
3602	6/51
3606	10/51
3607	9/53
3700	10/51
3702	4/53

(DISCOVERY)
10	1/49
107	9/49
120	1/50
127	2/50
131	4/50
132	5/50
134	7/50
147	5/51
500	1/49
502	2/49
503	3/49
504	5/49
507	9/49
517	1/50
518	2/50
519	6/50
520	7/50
528	9/50
534	2/51
2000	1/49

(GEM)
207	7/53
209	8/53
219	10/53

220	5/54
7001	7/53
7005	1/54

(GOSPEL)
1000	10/58
1004	11/58
1008	12/58
1014	2/59
1019	4/59
1021	6/59
1028	10/59

(KING SOLOMON)
1000	9/43
1003	1/44
1020	12/47

(REGENT)
107	10/47
109	11/47
111	12/47
112	3/48
117	5/48
121	7/48
122	8/48
125	9/48
133	10/48
142	3/49
153	5/49
158	6/49
173	3/50
174	5/50
183	12/50
185	2/51
187	9/51
188	10/51
190	2/52
195	5/52
196	1/53
200	1/54
1000	7/49
1002	8/49
1005	9/49
1006	10/49
1007	11/49
1009	1/50
1014	2/50
1018	5/50
1019	7/50
1021	8/50
1022	9/50
1023	10/50
1025	12/50

1028	1/51
1030	3/51
1038	6/51
1040	10/51
1041	11/51
1042	2/52
2000	9/48
2002	10/48
2003	12/48
7501	5/56
7504	9/56
7506	12/56
7507	12/58
8501	5/52

(ROYALTY)
300	5/50
308	10/50

SAXON
ZA-100	4/49

S.B.W.
2337	8/47

SCAMORE
110	10/59

SCARLETT
4000	9/59
4001	11/59

SCATT
1609	4/58
1612	6/58

SCENIC
806	7/58

SCEPTOR
1201	12/58
1204	8/59
1205	9/59

SCOOP

1001	6/47
1003	3/52

9000	6/49

SCOPE

101	5/59

501	10/58

1001	6/55

1102	11/58

1956	10/56
1957	1/57

SCORE
SEE ALADDIN

SCOOTER
SEE ROYAL
            ROOST

SCOTTIE

1302	5/59
1304	6/59
1307	7/59
1308	8/59
1310	10/59

SCOUP

9000	6/49

SCULLY

106	7/59

SEAFAIR

1000	4/56

SECURITY

106	10/57
107	2/58
108	7/58
109	9/58
110	10/58
112	6/59

SEECO

10-004	4/49
10-010	7/53

502	7/45
529	11/45
583	3/47
670	10/48
684	2/50

830	2/50
840	4/50

4119	6/49
4147	7/54
4151	8/54
4157	11/54
4164	4/55
4166	5/55
4176	10/55
4182	1/56

6004	6/58
6005	10/58
6018	3/59
6019	4/59
6030	6/59
6033	10/49
6034	11/59
6040	12/59

7031	2/50
7048	4/50
7050	8/50
7128	12/51
7212	7/52

SEGER

7001	6/52
7004	9/52
7006	11/52
7009	5/53
7013	6/53

SELECT

48	10/54

186	9/52

299	6/53

2503	4/49

SELECTIVE

101	4/49
103	5/49
104	7/49
108	10/49
109	12/49
114	1/50
115	2/50
116	3/50
119	5/50
121	6/50

XS-1XA	7/49
2X	3/50

SELEST

?	10/50

SENSATION

16	10/49
23	1/50
27	2/50
31	4/50
35	6/50

SENTRY

301	7/50

501	7/50

SENTRY

1067	4/59

SERENADE

100	7/47
101	8/47

500	10/49
506	5/52

723	11/54

SESION

1001	11/57

SESSION

701	10/59

SEVA
502   7/45

2005   12/47
2006   3/48
2008   7/48

SEVEN HILLS
1156   10/53

SEVILLE
102   11/59

SHAD
SEE CASTLE

SHAMMY
501   4/59

SHAMROCK
999   7/59

SHAMROCK
7016   4/54

SHAN-TODD
0055   1/59

SHAR
1   7/59
2   12/59
----
355   12/59

SHARP
S-2   7/49
30   3/51
32   6/51
34   8/51
38   9/51
39   10/51
47   5/52

SHASTONE
101   6/58
103   7/58

104   8/58

SHAWNEE
513   7/49

SHEEN
101   6/59

SHELL
711   12/58
715   12/59

SHELLY
1000   9/59

SHERATON
53   10/55

1001   11/54
1003   1/55

50959   7/54

SHERRA
1501   4/59

SHIELD
100   1/59

SHO-ME
501   1/51
514   7/51
515   5/52
527   10/52
----
839   5/53

SHOOP
1050   3/59

SHOWBOAT
1501   9/59

SHOWCASE
704   8/55

2101   8/53

SHOWTIME
1021   9/55

1104   12/54
1110   12/56

SHUBERT, FRANZ
SEE FRANZ S.

SIERRA
1502   6/59
1503   7/59

SIERRATEN
1002   10/56

SIGNATURE
107   4/47
144   8/47
162   9/49
----
233   10/49

1002   8/46
1003   1/47
1006   4/47
1011   6/47
1017   6/47
1020   7/47
1025   12/47
1027   4/48
1029   6/48

2001   1/47

12002   7/59
12006   9/59
12013   10/59
12014   11/59

15001   7/45
15006   11/45
15007   1/46
15016   3/46
15032   6/46
15034   8/46
15048   10/46
15061   1/47
15074   2/47

SIGNATURE
CON'T
15106	4/47
15127	6/47
15138	8/47
15157	9/47
15166	12/47
15175	1/48
15190	3/48
15205	5/48
15208	6/48
15210	7/48
15225	9/48
15240	10/48
15242	11/48
15243	1/49
15250	2/49
15261	4/49
15263	1/50
15265	2/50
15268	3/50
15273	4/50
15277	8/50
15288	11/50

28101	7/45
28119	1/47
28129	5/48

32001	10/48
32025	11/50

(HANOVER)
4500	5/58
4502	6/58
4504	7/58
4506	8/58
4509	9/58
4512	10/58
4516	1/59
4518	2/59
4519	3/59
4520	4/59
4526	6/59
4533	9/59
4537	10/59

SIGNET
251	3/59

SILHOUETTE
501	5/54
503	6/54
509	2/55

515	8/56
526	1/58

SILVER
103	1/50

SILVER
1002	11/59
1003	12/59

2001	12/57

SILVER LEAF
101	12/59

SILVER SPUR
101	8/46

SILVER STAR
101	2/48
102	11/48

SIM FONTA
502	4/50

SIMPSON
11301	2/59

SIMS
103	5/55
104	8/55
105	11/55
107	6/56
109	10/59

S.I.N.A.
507	10/59

709	10/59

SING
23001	5/59

SING-A-TUNE
79	5/48

505	3/48
515	5/48

SINGSPIRATION
3068	2/51

SINGTIME
1000	5/54
1002	6/54

1251	10/54

1500	12/54

SINGULAR
110	5/58

712	4/58
713	5/58

1007	8/57

1314	12/59

SIR
SEE BATON

SIROC
201	8/58

SIW
SITTIN'-IN
SEE CASTLE

SIX THOUSAND
601	10/57

SKATING
      RHYTHMS
SEE HOLLYWOOD
      RHYTHMS

SKIDMORE
772	8/57

SKIPPY
58   1/59
----
101   2/58
102   5/58
103   8/58

SKOOP
1051   9/59

SKYLARK
523   6/51
525   10/51
532   1/52
538   5/52
545   8/52
549   2/53
550   5/53
556   12/53

SKYLINE
2   8/48
----
68   10/48

SKYLINE
500   11/58
502   6/59
----
752   4/59

SKY MEJ
1   8/58

SKYROCKET
101   2/56

1002   3/59
1004   8/59

SKYSCRAPPER
1250   12/50

SKYSTREAK
1007   2/50

SKYWAY
101   12/53
103   5/54
111   11/55

SKYWAY
100   2/59
116   6/58
120   12/58

SLATE
3006   4/50
3011   11/50
3046   2/54

6027   2/50
----
800   1/50

8000   7/46
8001   9/46

SMART
321   9/59

1001   4/58
1007   8/58

SMART
711   11/53

1002   11/49
1016   5/52

SMASH
2001   10/57

SMC
1234   10/49
1256   1/50
1266   5/50
1277   10/50

SMOKE
101   9/59

SMOKEY
101   9/59

SNAG
101   4/59
107   6/59

SNAKE
69   6/58

SNOOKY PRIOR
8910   7/53

SNOWCAP
101   2/56

SOBIE
2333   8/47

SOCIETY
13   2/51
18   11/51

SO DESKA
111   3/56

SOLID GOLD
711   6/56
712   7/56
715   12/57

SOLO
10-001   2/49
10-006   3/49
10-014   12/49

12-006   7/49

SOLO
105   2/57
108   7/57

SOMA
1050   12/56
1085   11/57
1091   3/58

SOMERSET
SEE PALDA

SONATA
1051   6/50

SONGBIRD
100   10/47

SONGBIRD
201   2/56
207   6/57
----
306   10/56

1201   9/54

SONGCRAFT
100   12/49

SONG OF THE
          MONTH
1195   7/46

SONIC
601   2/57

SONORA
104   1/47
105   2/47
106   3/47
114   5/47
----
500   2/47

1059   6/44
1087   3/45
1165   3/47
1177   5/47
1195   10/47
1207   2/48

2000   2/47
2005   3/47
2015   6/47

3004   3/46
3025   1/47
3042   2/47

3047   6/47

5012   4/47

7021   1/47
7037   3/47
7044   5/47
7049   9/47
7051   10/47

SORORITY
SEE FRATERNITY

SOUND
503   8/57
----
109   1/55
112   3/55
114   4/55
126   11/55

6900   3/58
6909   11/58

SOUTHERN
104   2/46
124   3/46
125   4/46
127   1/47
132   3/47
(HARLEM)
1000   5/46
1010   3/47
1037   4/49
(CHICAGO)
106   8/45

SOUTHFIELD
4501   3/59
4502   4/59

SOUTHWEST
204   12/55
----
400   12/55

SOUVENIR
303   8/59

1002   7/53

SPACE
101   6/58

SPADE
1929   11/56
1930   1/57
1935   5/57

SPANGLE
2001   7/57
2010   9/58
2011   10/58

SPANN
402   2/59
415   3/59
431   6/59

SPARK
SEE ATLANTIC

SPARKLE
101   12/58

SPARTON
327   10/56

SPECIALTY
305   1/48
307   4/48
311   7/48
314   8/48
317   12/48
320   3/49
325   4/49
329   6/49
332   7/49
333   8/49
339   10/49
342   12/49
345   1/50
353   3/50
358   5/50
362   6/50
365   7/50
371   8/50
374   9/50
381   11/50
390   1/51

SPECIALTY						
CON'T		584	10/56	831	8/52
397	4/51	587	11/56	833	9/52
404	5/51	592	1/57	836	11/52
406	6/51	594	2/57	837	12/52
410	9/51	598	3/57	841	2/53
413	10/51	599	4/57	842	3/53
415	11/51	606	5/57	846	5/53
417	12/51	610	8/57	848	6/53
420	2/52	611	9/57	850	8/53
426	3/52	612	10/57	852	9/53
428	4/52	619	11/57	854	11/53
432	5/52	624	1/58	856	12/53
435	8/52	625	2/58	857	2/54
439	9/52	626	3/58	862	5/54
442	10/52	628	4/58	863	6/54
443	11/52	631	5/58	866	7/54
446	12/52	634	6/58	868	10/54
451	1/53	636	7/58	875	12/54
455	3/53	640	8/58	876	1/55
460	4/53	642	9/58	877	4/55
461	5/53	648	10/58	880	7/55
464	6/53	650	11/58	883	9/55
466	7/53	653	12/58	889	2/56
469	8/53	655	1/59	892	3/56
473	9/53	659	2/59	893	4/56
479	10/53	661	3/59	894	6/56
481	12/53	664	4/59	897	11/56
483	1/54	666	5/59	901	12/56
484	2/54	669	6/59	904	3/57
488	3/54	672	7/59	905	6/57
490	4/54	674	8/59	907	12/57
494	5/54	677	10/59	910	12/58
497	6/54	----------		912	3/59
499	7/54	500	8/46	914	4/59
527	8/54	505	11/46	919	10/59
530	9/54	513	3/47	----------	
535	10/54	518	8/47	(JUKE BOX)	
536	11/54	519	1/48	100	1/45
537	12/54	524	4/48	101	11/45
540	1/55	----------		----------	
544	2/55	701	1/49	502	11/45
546	4/55	705	7/52	503	1/46
551	5/55	708	11/52	505	4/46
554	7/55	714	5/53	508	8/46
555	9/55	715	7/53	510	9/46
557	10/55	----------		512	11/46
562	12/55	800	5/51	515	12/46
566	1/56	804	7/51	516	1/47
570	2/56	806	8/51	517	4/47
571	3/56	808	9/51	FIDELITY	
573	4/56	813	10/51	SEE PAGE 157	
576	5/56	815	12/51	SPEED	
579	6/56	817	2/52	703	3/59
580	7/56	821	3/52	704	9/59
582	9/56	826	4/52	----------	
		829	7/52	6865	6/58

SPHINX
1201　　8/59

SPIN
847　　9/45
858　　10/45

SPIN
2004　　12/53

SPINIT
101　　8/50

201　　8/50

5501　　2/55

SPINNER
99-1004　　1/49

SPINNETT
1001　　6/49
1002　　7/49

SPINNING
6002　　6/58
6005　　9/58
6006　　11/58
6007　　1/59
6009　　6/59

SPIRAL
800　　8/58

SPIRE
11-001　　6/49
11-003　　10/49
11-007　　4/50

103　　10/49

1001　　6/49
1002　　8/49

SPIRIT
104　　12/56

SPIRO
3001　　9/48

6002　　3/48

8001　　5/48

9009　　5/48

9511　　8/48

SPLASH
800　　3/59
802　　6/59

SPOT
014　　3/59

101　　3/59
104　　6/59
106　　7/59

5303　　9/58

SPOTLIGHT
387　　7/55
389　　10/55
393　　1/56
395　　3/56

SPOTLIGHT
500　　3/49
516　　4/49
521　　6/49

2001　　11/45
2006　　1/46
2007　　2/46

SPOTLITE
801　　3/53

SQUARE
101　　6/54

STACY
913　　5/59

STAFF
602　　12/47
606　　7/48
641　　12/49
646　　1/50

706　　12/49
707　　1/50

STAN
300　　11/58

STANDARD
100　　3/57

152　　1/50
153　　4/50
158　　5/50
174　　9/52

700　　6/58

770　　5/57

1000　　11/41
1003　　1/42
1008　　12/42

2001　　7/41
2009　　8/41
2019　　11/41
2029　　12/41
2045　　3/42
2056　　4/42
2058　　5/42
2060　　6/42
2076　　10/42
2077　　1/43
2087　　2/43
2091　　3/43
2101　　11/43
2106　　4/44
2110　　8/44

5000　　10/42
5004　　11/42
5005　　1/43

7012　　1/50

14004　　1/50

35000　　2/49
35003　　4/50

STAN-LEE
105   12/44

STANSON
501   9/58
502   11/58

STAR
56   9/56
----
171   1/55
----
805   9/58

STAR
210   8/46
----
417   1/48
----
602   4/49
604   5/49
610   8/49

1378   11/49

STARDALE
001   11/55
----
333   6/56
----
600   4/59

STARDAY
101   7/53
103   8/53
112   9/53
115   11/53
118   12/53
122   1/54
129   3/54
131   4/54
146   5/54
147   6/54
152   7/54
156   8/54
159   9/54
164   10/54
165   11/54
167   12/54
175   2/55
178   3/55

184   4/55
188   5/55
192   6/55
195   7/55
199   8/55
203   9/55
214   11/55
218   12/55
220   1/56
221   2/56
227   3/56
232   4/56
240   5/56
244   6/56
250   7/56
254   8/56
257   9/56
265   10/56
267   11/56
279   12/56
280   2/57
285   3/57
288   4/57
290   5/57
297   6/57
306   7/57
310   8/57
323   10/57
331   11/57
334   12/57
345   2/58
357   4/58
364   6/58
401   9/58
404   11/58
412   12/58
418   1/59
419   2/59
423   3/59
431   4/59
434   5/59
438   6/59
445   7/59
449   8/59
455   9/59
462   10/59
465   11/59
470   12/59
----
518   5/55
541   2/56
554   4/56
578   10/56
607   2/57
642   7/57
663   10/57

674   11/57

(DIXIE)
2001   2/58
2003   4/58
2005   6/58
2006   7/58
2010   11/58
2015   3/59
2017   5/59
2026   12/59

STARDISC
100   11/57

STARDUST
1001   11/53

STARFIRE
600   5/59

1015   9/57

STARFIRE
3000   8/45

STARITE
SEE STARLITE

STARLA
S-1   8/57
3   10/57
5   12/57
6   2/58
9   4/58
15   5/59

STARLAND
221   1/54
----
251   12/50

STARLIGHT
1001   1/57
1002   6/58
1004   10/58
1005   11/58

STARLITE
1361   2/55
1362   5/55
1369   6/55
1375   3/56
1376   6/56
1378   9/56

7927   3/54

STARO
001   5/58

STAR MAIDS
101   5/55

STAR MAKER
501   11/53

STAR MELODIES
1001   8/49

STAR OF DAVID
1505   7/50

STARR
100   12/45
----
211   3/47

STARS
504   4/56
540   12/56
543   6/57
546   7/57
551   10/57
553   12/57

4774   11/55

STAR SATELITE
1003   10/58
1008   1/59
1013   12/59

STARS OF
    HOLLYWOOD

1001   4/59

STAR TALENT
711   1/50
715   3/50
----
755   2/50
758   5/50
778   10/51
----
807   2/50
816   5/50

STAR X
502   12/57
505   6/58
506   8/58
516   9/59

STATE CALLA
116   9/56

1170   5/58

STATES
SEE UNITED

STELLA
1005   3/53

3030   6/55

STELLAR
1001   9/47
1005   1/48
1012   4/48
1015   8/48
1018   1/49
1019   3/49

STENTOR
101   7/59

STEPHENY
07   9/57
09   10/57

1805   11/57

1818   2/58
1821   3/58
1825   4/58
1827   5/58
1831   10/58
1833   1/59
1835   4/59
1836   6/59
1837   7/59
1839   11/59

7114   9/57

STERLING
100   11/45
102   12/45
----
201   1/47
204   2/47
208   4/47
210   5/47
214   11/47

1501   1/47
1504   9/47
----
801   9/47
806   4/48

2001   10/47
2022   6/48

3000   9/47
3003   11/47
3004   12/47
3008   1/48
3015   2/48
3023   6/48

4003   3/48

7001   3/46

STERLING
903   11/55

STEVEN
1001   4/59

STEVENS
103   5/59
106   8/59

STEVENS	
CON'T	
107	9/59
STINSON	
SEE ASH	
STOMPER TIME	
859	10/58
STORK	
1001	5/46
STORM	
455	6/58
STORZ	
101	11/59
STRAND	
1008	1/49
STRAND	
25001	6/59
25004	6/59
25005	7/59
25007	9/59
25008	10/59
STRATOLITE	
969	9/59
STREET	
802	2/50
STUDIO	
1002	2/59

9901	7/59
9903	12/59
STYLE	
621	4/58
622	11/58

STYLECRAFT	
503	3/51

5078	12/55
5100	12/56
STYLETONE	
100	7/53
101	5/57

5803	6/59
STYLO	
2102	4/59
2105	6/59
SUE	
700	4/57
701	6/57
702	1/58
703	4/58
704	5/58
706	6/58
707	9/58
708	10/58
709	11/58
710	1/59
711	2/59
712	5/59
713	6/59
715	8/59
SULLIVAN	
502	9/47
504	3/49
510	1/52
513	5/52
SULTAN	
1003	8/59
SULTAN	
1428	5/50

2501	6/46
SUMMIT	
101	4/58
102	6/58

103	8/58
104	9/58
107	12/58
108	1/59
109	4/59
111	8/59
112	8/59
113	9/59
SUMMIT	
16	2/50

105	5/50
SUN	
101	1/52
SUN	
140	8/47

940	3/47

1041	3/47

1422	1/48
1428	9/48
SUN	
178	3/53
187	8/53
188	9/53
189	10/53
191	12/53
193	1/54
195	3/54
200	4/54
201	5/54
205	7/54
208	8/54
210	10/54
213	11/54
214	1/55
216	4/55
217	5/55
223	8/55
224	10/55
229	1/56
238	4/56
239	5/56
243	6/56
244	7/56
245	9/56

140   SUNBEAM

SUN CON'T
250	10/56
258	12/56
260	2/57
264	4/57
266	5/57
270	6/57
271	8/57
280	11/57
283	1/58
288	2/58
290	5/58
298	6/58
302	8/58
304	10/58
306	11/58
311	12/58
313	2/59
315	3/59
318	4/59
322	6/59
323	7/59
325	8/59
326	9/59
333	11/59

(FLIP)
501   3/55

(PHILLIPS INTERNATIONAL)
3519	10/57
3521	2/58
3524	5/58
3526	6/59
3527	7/59
3530	10/58
3534	11/58
3537	2/59
3538	4/59
3540	5/59
3542	7/59
3544	8/59
3546	9/59

SUNBEAM
100	11/46
101	3/47
107	5/47

SUNBEAM
102	4/58
104	6/58
105	7/58

110	8/58
115	10/58
116	11/58
122	1/59
123	2/59
125	3/59
129	4/59
131	6/59

1786   8/59

SUNDANCE
201   7/59

SUNDOWN
102	1/58
105	7/58
107	9/58
108	10/58
112	11/58
114	1/59
117	3/59
119	5/59
122	9/59

SUN-KIST
7000   11/56

SUN-NEL
12692   11/57

SUNNYSIDE
3102   1/59

SUNRISE
2001	4/47
2007	7/47
2014	1/48

SUNSET
2008	12/55
2012	3/56
2015	6/56
2019	7/56

SUNSET TRAIL
1556   7/51

SUNSHINE
105   3/46

SUNSHINE
101	3/57
102	8/57

SUNSHINE
1001   12/53

2155   12/52

SUN STONE
101   9/50

SUNTAN
1112   6/56

SUPERB
500   7/49

600   5/49

SUPERDISC
113   9/46

1000	9/45
1010	12/45
1012	8/46
1018	10/46
1024	2/47
1026	3/47
1035	5/47
1036	7/47
1047	12/47
1052	1/48
1054	2/48
1055	3/48
1060	5/48

SUPERIOR
111	6/46
126	6/49

702   6/49

SUPERIOR
2202   8/54

SUPERIOR
CON'T
3301   4/57

SUPREME
102   5/48

1500   5/48
1504   7/48
1507   10/48
1509   12/48
1511   2/49
1512   3/49
1515   4/49
1523   5/49
1527   7/49
1530   9/49
1532   10/49
1545   11/49

SUPREME
101   2/58

SURF
5016   10/57
5018   11/57
5019   12/57
5027   9/58
5036   6/59

SUTTON
1001   9/51

SWADE
104   8/58

SWAN
4001   12/57
4005   3/58
4006   4/58
4007   5/58
4010   6/58
4013   9/58
4020   11/58
4023   12/58
4026   2/59
4028   3/59
4031   5/59
4034   6/59
4038   8/59

4043   11/59
4047   12/59

SWAN
7514   1/47

8000   12/46
8002   1/47

SWANK
506   5/46

SWCI
100017   2/50

SWEETHEART
100   5/51

SWEET TONE
111   5/51

SWING BEAT
SEE DOWN BEAT

SWING MASTER
12   3/49
17   5/49
20   6/49
23   7/49
26   9/49

1010   12/49

SWING TIME
SEE DOWN BEAT

SWINGIN'
614   3/59
618   9/59

SYCAMORE
103   6/58

SYLVAN
350   2/49

354   6/49

SYMBOL
901   1/59
902   6/59
903   8/59
906   11/59

SYRENE
1280   5/50

TABB
1008   1/57
1009   3/57
1013   6/57

TAD
0711   5/59

TAGG
502   3/59
504   4/59

TALENT
252   2/59

TALENT
500   2/49
----
703   4/49
737   6/49
747   9/49
748   10/49
----
802   4/49
804   6/49
805   8/49

1001   2/49
1002   12/49

(DOUBLE
   FORTUNE)
2000   2/49
2010   4/49

TALLY
101   5/56
103   7/56
104   9/56
107   6/57
110   8/57
112   11/57
117   1/58
122   5/58

TALOS
405   8/59
----
500   9/58

TAMMY
1003   9/58
1005   3/59

TAMPA
101   2/55
102   5/55
107   9/55
109   2/56
112   5/56
116   8/56
121   9/56
122   2/57
127   7/57
138   4/58
142   6/58
160   12/58
162   2/59

2000   1/55

T & M
105   1/53
107   3/54

TANKER
715   8/59

TANNER 'T'
          TEXAS
1006   12/53

TARA
101   3/58

TARTAN
501   4/56

TAXCO
3002   2/48

TAYLEE
202   2/48

TAYLOR
250   9/53

TAYLOR
801   7/59

TAZ
1002   5/57
1003   7/57

9105   3/57

TEAL
10-1100   5/53

TECH-ART
500   6/46

TEE
1001   4/59

TEE GEE
101   7/58
105   9/58

TEEN
103   4/55
105   5/55
107   8/55

TEEN
507   7/59

TEEN-AGE
101   2/56

601   6/56

1001   6/56
1004   7/56

TEEN AGER
101   2/59
----
601   4/59

1001   5/59

TEENERAMA
1001   11/57

TEENS
505   6/59

TEK
1001   9/58
1002   11/58
1013   8/59

TEL
or TELL
1003   4/59
1004   5/59
1008   8/59

TELEFUNKEN
4501   5/59
4503   9/59
4504   11/59

18935   6/59

TELL
SEE TEL

TELL
5001   5/51

TEMPO
0276   10/52
----
544   2/47
574   7/47

TEMPO
CON'T
586	3/48
626	5/48
652	9/48
668	12/48
688	3/49
698	7/49

1034	9/47
1050	3/48
1060	12/48
1077	9/49

4730	3/50

TEMPUS
1509	2/59
1510	3/59
1513	8/59

7541	3/59

TENDER
510	5/58
513	6/58
515	9/58
518	2/59
521	6/59

TENNESSEE
SEE REPUBLIC

TERP
153	11/57

0518	3/58

TERRIFIC
151	12/58

TERRY
102	10/59

TERRY TUNES
161	4/56

TETRA
4444	9/56
4450	4/57

TEX
102	1/55
105	3/57

TEXADISC
1008	12/51

TEX-STAR
3	9/48

T-5	10/48
T-9	7/49

200	9/49

2158	7/48

THEME
100	8/50
142	4/51
152	7/51

THERON
102	3/52
103	2/54
112	8/55
114	10/55
117	1/56

5001	3/52

THOR
101	3/59
103	9/59

3 DUECES
505	11/49
507	2/50

3 MINUTES
SEE MILTONE

THRILLERS
170	9/53

THRILLWOOD
102	6/50
105	11/50
107	3/51
108	4/51

THUNDER
104	6/59

1021	8/59

THUNDERBIRD
19552	1/55

1955	3/55
1956	11/56
1957	12/58

THUNDERBOLT
811	3/59

TIARA
156	4/56
157	8/56

6001	7/55
6003	11/55

6101	4/57
6106	8/57
6108	10/57
6111	2/58
6114	3/58
6117	6/58
6119	8/58
6121	12/58
6123	1/59
6124	2/59
6125	3/59
6126	4/59
6127	6/59
6129	9/59

TICO
10-068	12/51
10-087	1/52
10-108	3/52

TICO CON'T
10-124	5/52
10-129	9/52
10-163	6/53
10-189	9/53
10-208	1/54

229	9/54
248	4/55
257	5/55
264	7/55
273	9/55
276	11/55
345	2/56
367	7/56
388	2/57
412	4/58

1093	10/54

(RAMA)
1	3/53
2	5/53
5	6/53
26	12/53
29	4/54
65	2/55
100	6/55
165	9/55
171	11/55
179	12/55
185	2/56
194	3/56
195	4/56
198	6/56
202	9/56
208	10/56
211	11/56
216	12/56
218	1/57
219	3/57
229	5/57
231	7/57

(GEE)
1	4/54
3	5/54
7	6/54
12	10/54

1000	12/55
1002	2/56
1004	3/56
1012	4/56
1014	5/56
1016	6/56

1018	7/56
1022	9/56
1023	10/56
1025	11/56
1027	1/57
1031	2/57
1033	3/57
1034	4/57
1037	5/57
1038	7/57
1040	9/57
1044	10/57
1046	12/57
1047	1/58
1050	11/59
1053	12/59

TIFFANY
1303	11/53
1304	12/53
1305	6/54
1311	10/54
1314	4/55
1316	8/55
1321	6/56

2580	7/54

TIGER
837	11/57

TILT
6545	9/57

1101	4/58

TIME
SEE CASTLE

TIME
101	12/46
102	5/47
107	7/49
109	11/49
116	9/50

209	9/51

TIMELIGHT
3005	6/58

TIMELY
SEE APOLLO

TIN PAN ALLEY
104	6/53
142	1/56
154	3/56
175	1/57
181	3/57
183	4/57
204	12/57
208	3/58
209	5/58

TIP TOP
708	3/58
713	9/58

7130	12/59

TIP TOP
5002	5/51

TIP-TOP
202	11/55

1003	11/55

TITAN
1701	8/59
1702	11/59

TNT
108	1/54
109	2/54
114	4/54
115	5/54
117	9/54
119	2/55
120	3/55
122	5/55
125	6/55
129	8/55
130	10/55
131	2/56
136	7/56
142	10/56
145	3/57
146	4/57
151	5/58

TNT
160	12/58
162	3/59
164	6/59
170	7/59
174	8/59
175	11/59

1007	1/54
1009	3/54
1017	9/55
1019	5/56

5001	10/56

8004	10/54
8005	2/55

9005	2/56
9006	4/56
9010	5/57
9015	4/58
9019	4/59
9023	9/59

TODD
1000	12/57
1007	2/59
1011	3/59
1022	4/59
1024	5/59
1028	6/59
1033	7/59
1037	10/59
1038	11/59

104	10/59

TOKEN
100	12/49
101	4/50
106	4/51
112	1/52

200	12/49
201	3/51
205	8/51

303	10/50

TONAY
| 1200 | 11/53 |

TONE
1001	3/48
1119	9/56
1126	10/56

TONE-CRAFT
| 205 | 7/55 |

TONEX
| 2748 | 5/53 |

TONI
| 100 | 12/58 |

TOP
1144	2/45
1147	8/45
1148	12/45
1152	2/47
1154	8/47
1155	10/47
1159	12/47

TOPIC
| 8001 | 4/59 |
| 8002 | 7/59 |

TOPP
1001	11/58
1002	12/58
1004	3/59
1008	9/59

TOPPER
| 200 | 6/52 |
| 281 | 6/58 |

TOP RANK
2000	5/59
2004	6/59
2007	8/59
2014	9/59
2015	10/59
2022	11/59
2025	12/59

TOPS
| 307 | 10/59 |

TOPS
| 340 | 10/52 |

TOPSY
| 1001 | 11/58 |

TOP TEN
| 135 | 6/52 |

TOP "20"
| 101 | 6/57 |

TOP TUNE
| 423 | 10/50 |
| 426 | 11/50 |

TORCH
| 109 | 8/59 |

TORE
| 1006 | 3/59 |

TOWER
205	12/48

1247	2/47
1258	11/47
1272	12/47
1288	7/48

1486	7/48

2005	2/48

TOWN & COUNTRY
| 1004 | 5/55 |

TOWNHOUSE
| 3 | 7/59 |

TRACE
101   12/58

TRACK
1002   7/59

TRANS-CONTINENTAL
3000   3/59
3001   5/59

TRANSWORLD
100   7/48

TRANS-WORLD
SEE PALDA

TREASURE TONE
2582   1/55

TREAT
502   5/55
507   7/55

TRELL
1777   12/50

TREND
50   5/53
56   6/53
60   8/53
63   9/53
69   2/54
71   4/54
74   5/54
82   7/54
83   10/54

1152   5/53

2502   4/54

TREND
000X   1/58
----
002   2/58
005   3/58

007   4/58
008   5/58
010   6/58
013   7/58
016   11/58

30018   7/59

TREPUR
40   12/52
----
501   9/55
503   6/55

1002   6/57
1003   4/58
1004   5/58
1006   11/58
1008   12/58
1010   6/59

TREY
SEE ATLANTIC

TRIAL
7090   6/50

TRIANGLE
51315   9/59

TRIBORO
101   7/53

TRIBUTE
501   10/56

TRILON
116   4/46
118   5/46
122   6/46
124   10/46
143   12/46
183   8/47
190   1/48
203   2/48
205   3/48

12457   4/46

(RHYTHM)
108   7/46
----
201   8/46
----
303   8/49

1015   7/49

TRINITY
104   12/55
106   4/56

TRIPLE A
2504   2/53
2511   4/53
2527   12/53

TRIPLE D
797   12/56

TRI-STATE
101   8/48
113   9/48
116   10/48

TRI-TONE
1001   3/52
1007   9/52
1020   8/55
1022   10/55

TRIUMPH
600   1/59
602   2/59
605   3/59
606   4/59
607   6/59
609   7/59

TRIUMPH
811   9/50

TROJAN
20101   1/53

TROPE
202   6/48
----
777   2/49

TROPHY
500   9/58
502   1/59

TROPICAL ISLE
103   5/59

1008   6/59

4001   4/59

TROY
400   4/59

TRU-BLUE
106   6/48
120   10/48
----
415   6/54
----
500   1/49

TRUE-BLUE
VARIANT OF
ABOVE
201   11/48
----
302   12/48
----
504   2/49

TRUE-BLUE
113   7/55

TRUMP
501   1/59
----
817   1/59

TRUMPET
135   4/51
137   7/51
139   9/51

---

145   11/51
151   2/52
160   4/52
172   5/52
176   8/52
180   10/52
186   12/52
192   2/53
195   5/53
199   6/53
202   8/53
212   12/53
217   3/54
221   8/54
233   2/55
----
309   8/51
----
351   4/51

TUNE
202   5/57
206   7/59

TUNE-DISC
101   10/46
102   7/47

TUNE DISK
101   7/47

TUNE TONE
102   4/58

TURF
1000   8/59

TUXEDO
880   10/51
881   12/51
882   4/52
883   8/52
884   4/53
889   5/53
890   11/53
892   2/54
895   4/54
896   5/54
899   2/55
901   4/55

---

902   7/55
906   11/55
908   12/55
909   4/56
913   5/56
917   10/56
918   1/57
919   4/57
921   9/57
922   11/57
924   7/58
929   6/59
932   12/59

2502   2/53

20TH CENTURY
SEE GOTHAM

20TH CENTURY
           FOX
100   4/58
101   5/58
103   6/58
108   7/58
109   8/58
112   9/58
116   11/58
121   12/58
126   1/59
128   2/59
132   3/59
135   4/59
142   5/59
146   6/59
152   7/59
161   10/59
171   11/59

TWIN
101   6/59

ULTRA
SEE ALADDIN

ULTRA
151   8/46
----
710   1/47

UNART
SEE UNITED
            ARTISTS

UNICAL
101   7/56

UNIQUE
ALSO AS
RKO UNIQUE
302   4/55
304   5/55
307   6/55
310   8/55
311   9/55
323   12/55
324   1/56
325   2/56
328   3/56
333   4/56
336   5/56
340   7/56
345   8/56
353   9/56
363   10/56
370   11/56
373   12/56
388   2/57
390   3/57
395   4/57
398   5/57
403   6/57
404   7/57
414   8/57

UNITED
101   8/51
103   9/51
104   10/51
112   3/52
115   4/52
120   5/52
121   7/52
124   8/52
126   9/52
129   10/52
132   11/52
139   1/53
145   3/53
146   4/53
149   5/53
151   7/53
154   8/53

158   9/53
160   10/53
163   12/53
168   2/54
173   3/54
174   5/54
178   6/54
180   7/54
182   9/54
184   10/54
186   12/54
187   2/55
189   5/55
190   6/55
191   8/55
193   10/55
196   1/56
197   3/56
199   5/56
201   6/56
202   10/56
209   2/57
210   9/57
214   11/57

(B&F)
1321   6/59
1322   8/59
1325   9/59
1329   12/59

(STATES)
101   5/52
104   6/52
106   7/52
107   11/52
112   1/53
115   3/53
116   4/53
117   5/53
118   6/53
119   7/53
122   8/53
125   9/53
129   12/53
133   2/54
134   3/54
137   4/54
138   5/54
139   6/54
143   12/54
146   2/55
147   4/55
150   7/55
152   12/55
154   2/56

156   5/56
157   9/56
158   10/56
164   11/57

UNITED ARTISTS
100   9/47
----
401   11/47
----
610   11/47
----
703   1/48
----
901   11/47

UNITED ARTISTS
101   12/57
103   1/58
106   2/58
107   3/58
113   4/58
126   5/58
129   6/58
139   8/58
143   9/58
148   10/58
150   11/58
153   12/58
155   1/59
157   2/59
162   3/59
166   4/59
169   5/59
179   6/59
180   8/59
185   9/59
187   10/59
192   11/59

(UNART)
2002   9/58
2006   12/58
2009   2/59
2011   3/59
2017   6/59
2019   8/59
2023   9/59
2025   11/59

UNIVERSAL
25   12/47
31   1/48

UNIVERSAL
CON'T
47	2/48
114	5/48
122	10/48
142	4/49
147	5/49

| 850 | 9/47 |

| 7505 | 12/47 |

UNIVERSAL
101   2/56

| 230 | 7/57 |

| 4013 | 11/52 |

| 10158 | 10/58 |

UNIVERSAL
INTERNATIONAL
7422   6/59

UNIVERSAL
SHERATON
| 1007 | 4/55 |
| 1008 | 11/55 |

UNIVERSITY
25   1/47
- - - - - - - -
505	11/45
508	1/47
516	2/47

UNIVERSITY
8201   10/59

UPTOWN
100	12/48
120	3/49
126	5/49
- - - - - - - -
| 210 | 2/49 |

UP TOWN
757   3/59

URAB
13   3/48

| 505 | 1/48 |

URANIA
| 1002 | 4/57 |
| 1005 | 11/57 |

| 5005 | 7/59 |

| 9024 | 6/59 |

URBAN
| 112 | 2/46 |
| 123 | 6/46 |

U. S.
207   11/50

U. S. A.
| 403 | 3/54 |
| 406 | 5/54 |

U. T.
4000   6/59

UTOPIA
| 1954 | 5/56 |
| 1977 | 3/57 |

VACATION LAND
1   8/59

VALLEY
105	6/53
111	2/54
113	3/54

VALLEY
101   6/58

| 1005 | 10/59 |

VALOR
2003   11/58

| 2005 | 2/59 |
| 2006 | 3/59 |

VAL-UE
101   11/58

V & V
400   5/59

VANGUARD
35001	3/58
35003	4/58
35005	12/58
35007	9/59

VANITY
501	11/51
503	8/52
509	4/53
512	5/53
513	7/53
533	2/54
543	11/54
546	6/55
559	12/55
562	5/57

VARGO
29023   1/48

VARIETY
1007	4/58
1009	6/58
1012	10/58
1015	5/59
1017	9/59

VARIETY
1212   2/47
- - - - - - - -
| 2123 | 3/47 |

VARSITY
101	8/48
111	9/48
114	10/48
116	11/48
167	9/49

VARSITY

213	10/49
240	2/50
256	3/50
262	4/50
265	5/50

5001	8/48
5022	1/50
5141	10/51

8001	8/48
8018	10/49
8042	1/50
8056	3/50

8143	1/40
8167	2/40
8170	3/40
8259	4/40
8270	5/40
8312	6/40
8349	7/40
8398	8/40

(ELITE)

5006	1/42
5012	2/42
5016	3/42
5020	4/42
5022	5/42
5026	6/42
5031	7/42
5034	8/42
5038	9/42
5041	10/42
5046	11/42

(HIT)

1001	10/44
1010	1/45

7001	5/42
7003	6/42
7006	7/42
7012	8/42
7017	9/42
7018	10/42
7021	11/42
7026	12/42
7029	1/43
7036	2/43
7038	3/43
7040	4/43
7042	5/43
7047	6/43

7048	7/43
7052	8/43
7054	9/43
7056	10/43
7065	11/43
7069	12/43
7071	1/44
7075	2/44
7079	3/44
7083	4/44
7088	5/44
7096	6/44
7097	7/44
7105	8/44
7107	9/44
7111	10/44
7114	11/44
7119	12/44
7122	1/45
7125	2/45
7128	3/45

(MAJESTIC)

1014	8/45
1015	9/45
1018	11/45
1023	12/45
1025	1/46
1031	3/46
1037	4/46
1038	5/46
1047	6/46
1056	7/46
1057	8/46
1075	9/46
1083	10/46
1090	11/46
1103	1/47
1108	2/47
1116	3/47
1130	6/47
1164	8/47
1165	9/47
1171	10/47
1174	11/47
1178	12/48
1217	1/48
1226	2/48
1238	3/48
1241	4/48
1252	5/48

3001	4/46

5000	5/46
5003	8/46

5004	10/46

7129	3/45
7133	4/45
7137	5/45
7141	6/45
7145	7/45
7149	8/45
7154	10/45
7157	11/45
7160	12/45
7165	1/46
7168	3/46
7177	4/46
7183	5/46
7191	6/46
7197	7/46
7201	8/46
7207	9/46
7208	12/46
7209	1/47
7211	2/47
7217	3/47
7220	4/47
7225	5/47
7237	6/47
7249	7/47
7261	8/47
7269	10/47
7271	11/47
7275	12/47

9000	9/46

11000	7/46
11001	8/46
11002	9/46
11003	1/47
11024	11/47

12003	9/46
12009	2/47

VAUGHN

101	8/52

VEDDA

4004	9/59

VEE JAY

101	7/53
103	10/53
104	12/53

VEE JAY
CON'T

105	1/54
106	2/54
108	6/54
110	8/54
113	9/54
116	10/54
117	12/54
120	1/55
127	3/55
137	5/55
146	6/55
148	7/55
153	8/55
155	10/55
159	11/55
164	12/55
167	1/56
171	2/56
180	4/56
189	5/56
191	7/56
197	7/56
204	8/56
205	9/56
214	11/56
228	12/56
234	2/57
236	3/57
242	4/57
246	5/57
251	8/57
255	9/57
258	11/57
260	12/57
270	1/58
275	3/58
278	4/58
279	5/58
282	6/58
286	7/58
290	8/58
293	9/58
299	10/58
301	12/58
305	1/59
306	2/59
308	3/59
314	4/59
317	5/59
319	7/59
324	9/59
329	10/59
333	11/59

843	5/57
845	6/57
847	7/57
848	9/57
850	11/57
853	12/57
857	5/58
861	9/58
872	7/59
878	8/59
880	10/59

(FALCON)

1001	6/57
1004	9/57
1005	10/57
1006	12/57
1011	2/58
1012	5/58

(ABNER)

1014	8/58
1019	11/58
1024	1/59
1025	3/59
1026	4/59
1027	6/59
1029	8/59
1030	9/59
1032	11/59

VEE-EIGHT

1000	3/59

VEGA

100	6/51

452	9/53

1001	1/59

VEKO

730	1/59

VEL-A-TONE

796	9/59

VELLEY

1401	1/58
1403	11/58

VELOR

2005	1/59

VEL-TONE

502	3/47

VELVET

7	5/53

VELVET

101	8/48

201	4/49

302	5/49

VENA

100	9/57
101	4/58

VENT

4258	12/56

VENTURE

111	3/59

VENUS

101	9/54
103	11/54

VENUS

300	7/59

VERITONE

1001	1/52

2001	1/53

VERNON

177	8/52
178	5/53

184	5/50

VOD-VIL	
424	12/51
VOGUE	
501	4/45

707	5/46
734	7/46
758	8/46
767	10/46
772	12/46
779	1/47
VOGUE	
1016	11/52
1017	2/53
1020	3/53
1022	4/53
1031	7/53
VOGUE	
8159	5/57
VOLCANO	
1	8/59
VOLK	
104	9/58
VOSS	
1010	6/59
VOX	
303	8/47

691	12/47

16058	5/47
V-TONE	
202	4/59
205	10/59
VULCAN	
137	6/59

1026	8/55

VULCAN	
5001	3/48
VULCO	
1500	10/58
1501	2/59
1515	8/59
WAGON	
1002	4/58
WALDORF	
101	12/49
WALDORF	
MUSIC HALL	
217	6/55
WAND	
102	12/59
WANDERLUST	
1109	2/59
1111	6/59

2008	8/56
2010	12/56
2098	1/59
WANGER	
SEE BERGEN	
WARNER	
1017	2/59
1021	6/59
WARNER	
	BROTHERS
5001	9/58
5011	10/58
5016	11/58
5022	12/58
5030	1/59
5036	2/59
5046	3/59
5052	4/59
5056	5/59

5073	6/59
5078	7/59
5090	8/59
5110	10/59
5122	11/59
5137	12/59
WARRIOR	
501	1/57
502	9/57
505	7/59
507	7/59

1554	5/58
WARWICK	
500	3/59
503	4/59
505	6/59
509	7/59
517	11/59
519	12/59
WATCO	
2140	11/54

111-11	3/55
111-13	11/55
WATTS	
5599	6/58
WAX	
103	8/47
WAYSIDE	
WAY-SIDE	
100	12/56
103	6/57

150	12/57
W. D.	
105	3/57
WEB	
1054	12/55
1057	2/56

WEB
CON'T
1060   4/56
1082   7/56
1101   3/57
1113   7/57
1118   2/58
1123   4/58

WEBSTER
502   9/49
506   4/50
510   7/50
515   10/50

WEEREBEL
WE RE BEL
100   9/58
101   10/58

WELLS
1   7/58

WEN DEE
1930   7/55
1934   12/55

WEST COAST
105   2/47

WESTERN
1110   11/45

WESTERNAIRE
101   10/47

4003   10/45

WESTERN
          CARAVAN
901   11/52

WESTMINSTER
7   12/58

4501   9/58
4503   1/59

WESTPORT
41   5/55
----
125   11/54
127   5/55
129   12/55
132   9/56
133   10/56
134   1/57
135   2/57
137   10/57
138   11/57
139   3/58
140   9/58
142   2/59
143   10/59

2495   2/59

WESTWIND
1   9/59
----
201   9/59

WESTWOOD
200   8/59

WHEELER
101   11/52

WHEELING
1150   11/53

WHEELING
SEE PALDA

WHIMSY
241   5/47
243   6/47
----
821   9/47

WHIPPET
100   3/56
----
200   3/56
201   6/56
203   11/56
206   3/57

212   1/58
213   4/58
----
250   2/57

WHIRL
103   11/58

WHIRL
121   5/52

WHIRLAWAY
75-2   7/48

WHIRLING DISC
SEE FURY

WHIRLWIND
105   12/58

WHISPERING
          PINES
200   9/59

WHITE CHURCH
1180   5/48

WHITEHALL
3001   8/59
3002   9/59
3003   10/59
3007   11/59

WHITE ROCK
1111   3/58

WHITE SQUIRREL
100   7/53

WHITE STAR
102   3/59

WHIZ
ALSO WHIZZ
ALSO WIZZ
711   9/58
712   10/58
714   12/58
715   1/59
716   5/59
717   6/59

1500   4/57

WIG
103   9/59
104   10/59

WIG-WAG
101   7/58

WILD
100   10/58

WILDCAT
0016   8/59
  18   10/59
0028   11/59

WILLET
0637   1/57

WILLIDA
4   10/47

WILLOW
1001   3/58
1002   6/58

WIL ROW
204   10/57

WIN
702   8/58

WINDOW
1006   8/57
1009   9/57

1113   2/58
1114   4/58
1117   11/58

5000   4/58

8574   11/57

WING
SEE MERCURY

WINLEY
215   3/57
219   6/57
220   8/57
224   2/58
237   2/59

WINSPIN
51   9/58

WINSTON
1014   6/57
1017   8/57
1019   11/57
1021   1/58
1022   7/58
1025   9/58
1027   11/58
1028   12/58
1029   1/59
1030   4/59
1031   5/59
1039   9/59

WIZARD
1002   6/59

WONDER
100   9/49

WONDER
102   7/58
105   9/58
108   10/58
109   12/58
112   4/59
114   6/59

WORD
150   11/53
----
503   10/53
----
652   11/53
677   5/54
686   8/59

WORLD
1501   8/48
1507   9/48
1508   12/48
1511   2/49
1518   6/49
1520   7/49

2501   10/48
2504   11/48
2509   4/49
2512   6/49

WORLD
1001   7/59

WORLD PACIFIC
646   3/58
649   6/58
650   8/58
----
801   1/59
802   4/59
803   9/59
804   10/59
806   11/59

WORLD WIDE
100   8/46

WORLD WIDE
2501   12/58

WORLD WIDE
SEE SAVOY

WREN
301   4/59
302   6/59

WRIGHTMAN
1010	5/47
1038	10/50
1057	9/51
1079	5/52

WRIMUS
701	1/57

WYN
1601	2/59
1602	6/59

WYNNE
101	3/59
104	4/59
105	5/59
109	6/59
114	7/59
116	8/59
117	9/59

X
SEE RCA

X-POWER
1001	3/59

XYZ
100	5/57
102	9/57
104	12/57
105	3/58

601	3/59
605	11/59

2001	8/58

YORK
70	4/59

101	11/55
111	1/56
113	3/57

3333	7/58

YOUR
1001	1/48

YUCCA
102	10/58
103	11/58
105	2/59
106	3/59
108	4/59
110	5/59
111	6/59
114	8/59
116	9/59

ZEBRA
23	6/57

118	12/57
120	4/58

700	7/59

ZEN
100	11/54

ZENITH
1042	7/50

ZEPHYR
501	3/56

3118	1/57

70-001	10/56
006	11/56
008	12/56
012	2/57
014	3/57
017	4/57
019	5/57

ZERO
101	10/59

ZEST
101	8/59

ZIPP
11208	9/56

ZODIAC
101	2/53
102	4/53
103	7/53
104	10/53
107	3/54

ZOE
100	12/53

ZOOM
102	11/56

001	3/59
002	5/59
004	9/59

ZZ
600	4/59

Addendum

BRUNSWICK
SEE DECCA

CENTER
SEE DERBY

CENTRAL
SEE DERBY

DECCA
(BRUNSWICK)

80214	2/53
80216	3/53
80217	4/53
80219	5/53
80221	7/53
80223	8/53
80227	9/53
80230	10/53
80233	11/53
80235	12/53
80236	2/54
80239	4/54
80241	5/54
80244	11/54

84002	2/53
84004	3/53
84007	4/53
84009	5/53
84011	6/53
84015	8/53
84018	9/53
84022	10/53
84024	11/54
84025	3/54

84026	4/54
84029	5/54
84031	6/54
84032	10/54

86000	7/53

DERBY
(CENTER)

101	12/53
102	6/54

(CENTRAL)

203	5/54

1003	5/53
1004	2/54
1005	3/54

EXCLUSIVE
SEE EXCELSIOR
IN MAIN TEXT

FIDELITY
SEE SPECIALTY

ROOST
SEE ROYAL
       ROOST
IN MAIN TEXT

SPECIALTY
(FIDELITY)

2001	12/51

3000	12/51
3002	2/52
3005	4/52

About the Compiler

WILLIAM R. DANIELS is Minister of the First Congregational Church of Salem, New Hampshire. He has published a number of articles in *Record Exchanger* and *Whiskey, Women And. . . .*